ISLAMIC ART
AND ARCHITECTURE

ISLAMIC ART
& ARCHITECTURE

BY

ERNST KÜHNEL

TRANSLATED BY

KATHERINE WATSON

CORNELL UNIVERSITY PRESS
Ithaca, New York

Originally published in 1962 as
Die Kunst des Islam
by Alfred Kröner Verlag of Stuttgart

English translation
Copyright © 1966
G. BELL AND SONS LTD
York House, Portugal Street
London, W.C.2

First published in the United States of America 1966
Cornell University Press

Library of Congress Catalog Card Number: 66–19223

Printed in Great Britain

Contents

5

Plates

9

Plans

Glossary

Bab	gateway
Fonduq	(1) an inn for travellers; (2) warehouse for merchants, especially those of Europe (cf. Italian 'fonidaco')
Hammam	steam bath
Haram	prayer hall, sanctuary
Harim	Arabic: literally 'forbidden'; applied particularly to women's apartments and their occupants
Hira	camp
Iwan	a very large niche looking on to an open court
Kamkha	damask
Kursi	a lectern for the Qur'an, often a hexagonal table
Kuttab	school
Madrasah	a college often with mosque attached, for the teaching of the Muslim religious sciences
Maghreb	the western region of Islam, viz. North Africa excluding Egypt. In the Middle Ages, Spain (*al Andalus*) was also included in the Maghreb
Mandara	room for reception of male guests
Maqsura	the part of the sanctuary of the mosque reserved for the ruler or governor
Mashribiya	window of wooden latticework
Mihrab	a niche incorporated in the wall of the sanctuary of the mosque to indicate the qibla (q.v.)
Minbar	pulpit
Moristan	hospital
Mudejar	Muslim under Christian rule
Musalla	open sanctuary
Okel	inn and warehouse for merchants
Qa'a	reception hall
Qamriya	a window tracery composed of coloured glass
Qasba	citadel
Qibla	the direction towards which the faithful must turn when reciting the ritual prayers; that is towards the sanctuary of Mecca; by extension, the wall of a mosque which indicates this direction
Quaisariya	complex of shops, workshops and warehouses which form a bazaar

15

Qubba	a dome; by extension a domed building, often housing the tomb of a saint
Rahle	a collapsible lectern for a book which when set up has the form of the letter X
Ribat	stronghold of monastic knights
Sebil	fountain
Sirdub	(Persian: literally cold-water) an underground room for use in hot weather
Suq	bazaar
Turbe	mausoleum
Yam	a post house or relay station

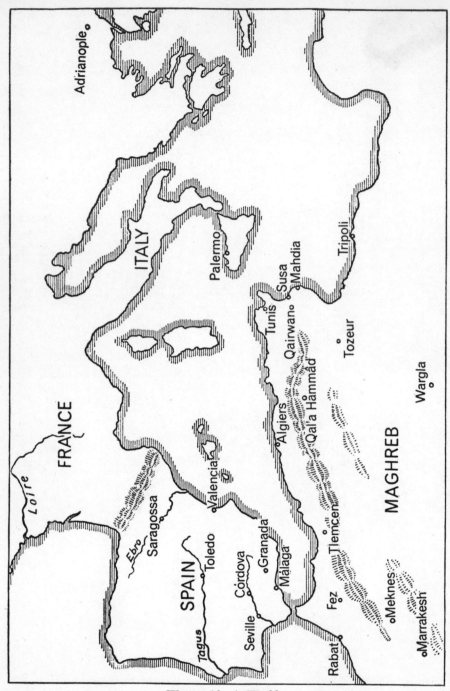

Western Islamic World.

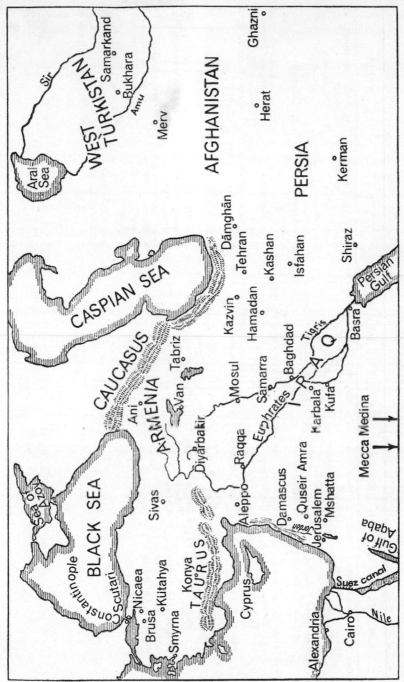

Eastern Islamic World.

CHRONOLOGICAL TABLE

CALIPHATE	SPAIN	NORTH AFRICA	EGYPT	SYRIA
632 Orthodox Caliphs Capital at Medina	710 Arab conquest of Spain	669–800 Governors appointed by Caliphs	641 Arab conquest of Egypt, Ummayad and Abbasid Governors	635 Arab conquest of Syria
656 Capital at Kufa	756 Ummayads of Cordova			661 Ummayads
661 Ummayad Caliphs Capital at Damascus	961 Hakam II	800 Aghlabids of Tunis	868–904 Tulunids (Turkish)	749 Abbasids
749 Abbasid Caliphs		909–972 Fatimids Capital at Mahdiye		877–1076 Tulunids and Fatimids of Egypt (909 Fatimid conquest of Sicily until 1071)
754 Mansur	1056–1148 Almoravids (Berbers)	972–1148 Zayrids of Tunis Capital at Qairawan	969–1171 Fatimids (Shi'ite) 969 New capital of Cairo	
762 New Capital at Baghdad				
786 Harun ar-Rashid	1130–1269 Almohads of North Africa			
833 Mu'tasim	1232–1492 Nasrids	1007–1152 Hammadids of Algeria	1169–1250 Ayyubids	1076–1176 Seljuks and Atabegs
836 New capital at Samarra	1492 Granada falls to Ferdinand and Isabella of Castille	1056–1148 Almoravids 1130–1269 Almohads	1250–1516 Mamluk Sultans (Slaves of Turkish origin)	1176–1271 Ayyubids
		1228–1534 Hafsids of Tunis	1293–1340 Nasin ad Din Muhammad ibn Qalaun 1468 Qait-Bey	1271–1516 Mamluk Sultans of Egypt (Wars with Crusaders and Mongols) (1446–1516 Tahirids in Yemen)
1258 Conquest of Baghdad by Hulagu: end of eastern Caliphate of the Abbasids			1560–1805 Ottoman Sultans of Turkey	1516 Ottoman Sultans of Turkey

MESOPOTAMIA	IRAN	TURKEY & ASIA MINOR	INDIA
635 Arab conquest of Iraq	642 Overthrow of Sasanids	1077–1327 Seljuks of Rum Capital at Konia	711 Arab conquest of Sind
661 Ummayads	661–819 Ummayad and Abassid Governors		962–1186 Ghaznavids
749 Abbasids	819–1055 Iranian dynasties	1300–1924 Ottoman Sultans	1100–1215 Ghorids of Afghanistan and Hindustan
1055–1262 Seljuks and Atabegs	819–1044 Samanids in Transoxiana and Iran	1299–1326 Uthman	1206–1555 Sultans of Delhi
1055 Capture of Baghdad by Tughril Beg	820–874 Tahirids in Khorasan	1326–1360 Urkhan Capital at Brusa	1391–1572 Kings of Gujarat
		1360–1389 Murad I	
1127–1262 Zangids (Atabegs of Mesopotamia and Syria)	854–1032 Aiids in Mazandaran	1365 Capital moved to Adrianople	1526–1858 Moghul Emperors
	868–903 Saffarids		1526 Babur Capital at Agra
1101–1232 Ortukids (Atabegs of Amida)	932–1055 Buwayids in South Iran and Iraq	1453 Capture of Constantinople Capital at Constantinople	1530–1556 Humayun (Refugee in Rian 1540–55)
1256–1336 Il-Khans of Iran	1037–1194 Seljuks		1556–1605 Akbar (Capital at Fathpur Sikri, then at Lahore)
1258 Overthrow of Caliphate	1037–1063 Tughril Beg	1481 Bayazid II	
	1206–1255 Great Khans	1520–1566 Sulayman I	
	1206–1227 Genghis Khan	1623–1640 Murad IV	1605–1628 Jehangir
1336–1502 Jalairids and Turkomans of Azerbaijan)			1628–1658 Shah Jehan
			1658–1707 Aurangzeb
1502–1628 Safavids of Iran			
1638–1918 Ottoman Sultans of Turkey			

Second portion of IRAN column:

IRAN
1256–1353 Il-Khans of Iran
1256–1265 Hulagu
1282 Ahmed Khan embraces Islam
1314–1393 Muzaffarids
1370–1500 Timurids
1370–1404 Timur. Capital at Samarkand
1453 Capture of Constantinople Capital at Constantinople
1502–1736 Safavids
1502–1524 Isma'il I
1587–1628 Abbas I
1628–1642 Safi
1648–1666 Abbas II

Introduction

THIS survey of Islamic art attempts to characterize the different styles which arose at various times and places; it is therefore desirable to set out by defining a few of the factors general to the whole development, which stress the unity transcending differences of region and period.

The cultural activity of the various peoples composing Islam was more strongly affected by their common possession of a religious confession than was the case in the Christian world; it bridged differences of race and tradition, and even forced the customs and manners of its components, as well as their spiritual concerns, into an extraordinarily clear and uniform mould. This process of assimilation was helped most of all by the importance of the Koran as a guide in all life's questions as well as in matters of faith; its propagation in the original language made the absolute supremacy of the Arabic script a bond which held the whole Islamic world together. The script was itself an important element in all artistic creation.

The contrast between sacred and secular art, as known in the West, was insignificant. Of course the cult buildings have their own particular architectural forms, mainly dictated by practical considerations, but their decoration is carried out no differently from that of secular buildings, and they have a minimum of special requirements compared with the liturgical apparatus of the Christian church. These requirements are limited to the prohibition of representations of living creatures, which were everywhere scrupulously avoided in religious places, although they occur more frequently elsewhere than is commonly realized. But even in the periods of greatest tolerance a pious decorum prevented the development of any outspokenly realistic leanings, and saw to it that the motifs drawn from nature were treated in an exclusively decorative manner. It would be a mistake to attribute symbolic or allegorical meaning to these natural motifs when they appear in fantastic stylizations, nor should one seek for the representation of historical events, however suggestive the scenes. Revulsion from naturalism suits so completely the temperament of Islamic man that even without the express warnings of the Prophet it would have made itself felt; it was strong enough to hinder the free and independent development of the arts of painting and sculpture as they are known elsewhere.

Hence the activity of the Islamic craftsmen was confined to works of architecture and applied art, and even in architecture the same decorative intentions which were operative in the minor arts determined the course of events, and lent enhanced importance to the decorative function of a building in space. For this reason it is entirely proper, and, in fact, essential for an understanding of the whole style, to give as much attention to ornament as to structure when studying the different phases of development. Without great painting and sculpture to lead artistic thought as it did in Europe, there was every reason why applied art should be raised from a subservient role. It provided work of extreme refinement of technique and expressiveness of form.

Building and crafts all depended entirely on encouragement by commissions from princes and other potentates, and every specially brilliant period is due to the quality of the patronage of the time. The monuments themselves record in inscriptions the importance of this protection, and when we come to ascribe them to various styles it becomes plain that the nationality of the artist counted for less than the attachment of the patron to one or another sphere of culture. It is hardly possible to speak of a separate Arabic, Persian, Turkish or Indian style within Islamic art; the prince's pleasure set the tone, deciding him to summon architects and craftsmen from the most distant regions to carry out his plans as quickly as possible; and whether they served religious or secular ends it was always imperative that the tasks be done in the shortest possible time. However advanced in years the ruler might be, if he endowed a mosque, built himself a palace or commissioned some outstanding piece of craftsmanship, his greatest concern was to live to see its completion. A building to be toiled at, generation after generation, had no appeal to the Islamic temperament, and it is surprising to read in ancient reports how short a period was often allotted to the artists for a commission, and how they generally fulfilled their work within it, though frequently, too, work which was begun lay unfinished.

In spite of all political divisions the Muhammadan states maintained considerable contact among themselves throughout the Middle Ages; this ensured lively trade and a constant exchange of spiritual goods, which had its effect on the work of designers and craftsmen; the travel reports of the great Arabic geographers demonstrate how much each country was informed of the merits of the others. It should not, therefore, be a matter for surprise that technical advances and artistic ideas were disseminated exceedingly quickly, and that stylistic affinities arose with an intensity which often bears little relation to the geographical proximity of the centres involved.

The reader, if he is schooled in Western views of art, needs to realize that Islamic art rests on premises which may at first seem alien. Architecture was completely 'earth-bound', and entirely horizontal in conception. Thus more than one building period always implies extension in breadth, and not increase in height. This can be seen more clearly in the palaces than in cult buildings, except in the cases where a new ruler preferred simply to build a new residence instead of enlarging that of his predecessor. How little the vertical concept prevailed can be seen in the way that tower buildings in all their manifold development never reached beyond a relatively modest height. 'Heaven-storming' buildings such as were built in the Christian world remained quite alien to Islam, and it is very rare that an outstandingly tall minaret dominates the silhouette of a town panorama.

For the same reason monumentality in Islamic architecture is only a relative term. Large imposing frontages and stately façades were not customary, commanding portals are rare and even domes were toned down: they were broken up inside by rising tiers of niches, and outside they were decorated and accompanied with gracious towers so that they lost much of their weight. This is

true to a certain degree even of the massive cathedral of Constantinople, its foreign models notwithstanding. The ground plan arose
rather haphazard through a combination of individually conceived
parts, even though they were erected at the same time, and thus
it achieves its effect less by harmonious unity than by picturesque
grouping. Lastly, it must be remembered that the architects were
often at pains to draw attention away from structural and static
problems so as to give visual stress to the decorative element.

In architectural decoration, as in the minor arts, the aim was to
fill surfaces in such a way as to avoid strongly emphasized contrasts between ornamented surfaces and empty areas, and above
all single motifs must not attract attention; rows and repetitions
were used to give the most fluent possible general impression
without giving any plastic prominence to one element or another.
The principle of 'overall surface covering' best met this requirement.

The forms of objects were dictated by their use. There were no
ornamental objects without practical purpose; at the very least
this purpose had to be suggested. Animals in procession round the
body of a vessel were a favourite theme, and riders or seated
figures in continuous repetition were treated as the least considerable of the artist's conceits. Indeed, often the subjects were meta-
morphosed for decorative purposes. The more these animate
subjects were stylized or schematized away from nature the more
they suited the Islamic aesthetic. The same is true of plant forms:
unreal rosettes and palmettes were the preferred themes, and the
unnatural split-leaf scroll was invented as the ornament *par
excellence* to dominate Islamic art of all lands and times in the
thousand variations of the 'arabesque'.

An important factor in the general development was the seces-
sion of the Mahgreb (the West) from political association with
the Islamic Orient after the mid-8th century; after this time it
went its own way, though with transitory influences coming at
times from the East. North Africa and Spain thus developed their
own distinctive Moorish style in art with an independent viability
which always remains in evidence within the limits imposed by
Islam. Persia, too, was divided from the other Muhammadan

countries by sectarian differences. The country became attached early and quite exclusively to the Shi'a, which recognized neither the first three caliphs nor the 'Sunna', the tradition which, with the Koran, was accepted by orthodox Muslims as binding. This religious separatism favoured the survival of national Iranian elements in art, though these did not find their full expression until a later period. When other areas adopted the Shi'ite confession for a spell—as Egypt did under the Fatimids—there immediately sprang up a sympathy with Persia and a noticeable acceptance of its artistic influence. The authority of the Caliph has often been overrated; inside the Sunnite province it steadily diminished as time went on, and after the early period exercised no appreciable influence on artistic matters.

EARLY ISLAMIC ART

CHAPTER ONE

The Umayyad Style

T HE earliest successors of the Prophet inherited his scrupulous concern to avoid all superfluous luxury. Their religious and political strength grew year by year, but they deliberately abstained from giving it material expression in proud palaces or splendid temples. The year 661, however, saw the transfer of the Caliphate to the Umayyad family and its removal from Medina to Damascus, and with this removal came a decisive change. Here, in the ancient Syrian capital, it became imperative that the places of worship of the victorious faith should not present too sorry an appearance beside the magnificence of heathen temples and Christian churches. It was equally important to set up a court whose brilliance showed that under the Caliphs Damascus was no longer overshadowed by Byzantium. Thus the new state became the scene of great building activity. This was facilitated by continuing the Byzantine system of public service by which a levy of men and materials was imposed on all regions of the Empire. Greek, Syrian, Persian and Egyptian craftsmen contributed to the final expression of an orientalizing, Late Antique decorative style.

The new ideas of architecture and of decoration were disseminated by the generals and governors in the service of the Caliphs to all the lands won to the Faith. In 750 the dynasty was overthrown by the Abbasids, but by then these elements of style were so deeply rooted in the Far West, in Spain, that they ensured a stylistic continuity into the new Umayyad regime there, whereas in the East artistic styles developed along completely other lines.

For another 300 years Cordova, in conscious opposition to Baghdad, saw it as a duty to uphold the Damascus tradition; and thereby wrought a miracle of creation, producing works of art which are accounted among the most brilliant manifestations of Islamic civilization, although limited throughout this long period to a well-nigh exhausted repertory of ideas.

Mosque Architecture

The religious meeting places of the Muhammadans were at first designed solely with the purpose of protecting the congregation, large or small, from the inclemencies of the weather during the rite of corporate prayer. This rite involved rhythmical movements executed in concert in straight rows; the somewhat military character of these services had to be provided for in the spatial planning. Another essential was a fountain for ritual ablutions,

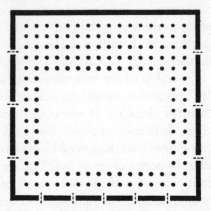

1. Reconstruction of the Ground Plan of the Mosque of Kufa according to the reports of the Arabic authors (after Creswell, *Early Muslim Architecture*, with a few alterations).

and the whole layout must be oriented towards the *qibla*, that is, towards Mecca. These practical requirements were satisfactorily met by the widely distributed older type of mosque with its inner courtyard (*sahn*) enclosed by galleries and a low, flat-roofed sanctuary (*haram*) with its aisles running parallel to the *qibla* wall (fig. 1). Memories of the Arab dwelling house and the example of the unwalled, open prayer place, already known in pre-Islamic times as the *musalla*, can both be seen to have influenced the arrangement. The earliest of these buildings were very modestly constructed of mud walls and palm trunks, roofed with mud-plastered palm leaves. Soon, however, the need arose for more solid construction; the necessary supporting material was provided from among the ruins of antique buildings, but the architect was now faced by a new and much wider set of problems. It is easy to see how the subsequent development towards monumental build-ing attached itself at first in some measure to the Christian basilica. Many basilicas in Syria were being converted into mosques. This was done by changing the focal point from the east end to the south wall, thus altering the axis from length to breadth. The introduction of a prayer niche (*mihrab*) to emphasize the Mecca wall is doubtless to be traced to the example of the choir apse, but the minaret (*manarah*, literally a light tower), which was allotted to the caller to prayer (*muezzin*) as a watch tower, is rather to be attributed to the signal towers surviving from earlier times, and partly also to the Palmyran funerary towers, than to the example of Syrian church towers. Once these substantial innovations were adopted, and accepted as necessary, there were further conse-quences dictated by architectural aesthetics, such as the broadening of the aisle running up to the niche and the placing of the tower in the centre of the opposite courtyard wall.

Most of the mosques erected by the Umayyads, both in the East and in the West, correspond to the type called by their name. Many of them were planned as garrison mosques of considerable dimensions, for the fighters of the Faith who had penetrated into newly conquered lands. Examples are those of Basra and Kufa in Mesopotamia (fig 1), that of Qairawan in North Africa (plate 2a), and the Mosque of 'Amr in Fostat, the earliest Muslim settlement in Cairo. This latter, built in 642 and enlarged as early as 673, had at first no *mihrab* and no inner courtyard, and was only later given the great pillared hall with its open courtyard (plate 1b), so im-pressive because of its enormous and completely plain undecor-ated space. It was the model for several Alexandrian mosques which have now disappeared. The mosque at Medina arose via numerous conversions and additions from the dwelling house of

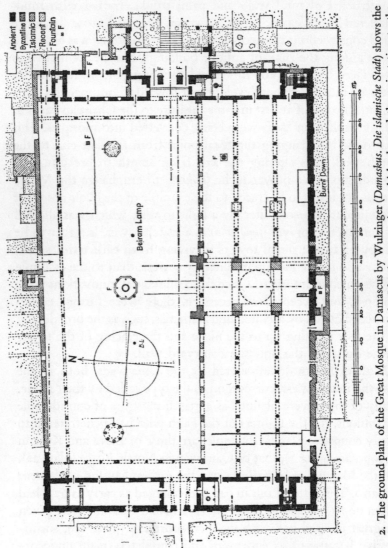

2. The ground plan of the Great Mosque in Damascus by Wulzinger (*Damaskus. Die islamische Stadt*) shows the antique *temenos*, the Byzantine basilica and the Islamic conversion, which changed the orientation to the south, and added a broad forecourt and minaret, also some later additions.

the Prophet himself which sufficed him as a cult centre during his lifetime. It was first set up on a monumental scale by the Caliph al-Walid in 712, and became the prototype of the pillared mosque with courtyard; as a pilgrimage centre it had great influence on further developments.

In Damascus itself the Umayyad mosque grew from the Church of St John, which at first the Muslims simply shared with the Christians. In 705 it was rebuilt as a pillared hall of three aisles with two-tiered rows of arches, transept and wooden roof. At this time the northern minaret was also added to the outside of the wide courtyard; its cubic shape, with the similar but smaller top (fig 2, plate 1a), is typical of the first period. Again at the 'Aqsa mosque in Jerusalem parts of a church of the time of Justinian were used, and here too the emphasis on the centre of the hall inspired the concept of a broad transept with a cupola, with seven more aisles added on each side, giving an impressive sense of depth. It was finished in 702, but rebuilt as early as 780, and subsequently it underwent many alterations. A *maqsura* (prince's box) was screened off under the cupola, a feature later found regularly beside the *mihrab*.

The Zituna mosque in Tunis (732) was closely similar in plan to Damascus, and is supposed to be the work of a Syrian architect. The famous mosque of Sidi 'Uqba in Qairawan, rebuilt shortly afterwards, must also have used the same model. The nave leading to the niche is broadened and domed at either end, and the unusually heavy minaret (plate 2a) lies on the same axis beyond the courtyard; this is enclosed by an arcade on piers faced with double columns. Even the Umayyad mosque at Cordova, which was not begun until 785, kept strictly to the Syrian design, both for its original layout and for the first two extensions (840 and 965), until in 990 for the final alterations the circumstances of the terrain dictated a departure from the axial principle in favour of an extension on one side only (fig 3). Here the horseshoe arch, evidently taken over from the Visigoths, was used throughout in place of the otherwise usual round arch. It appears in two tiers joined by short square pillars and enlivened by the contrasting colours of alternating stone and brick, in the gigantic sanctuary, a veritable forest of columns (plate 3). It developed simultaneously at this site into the trefoil and polyfoil cusped arch, and was also used for the first time in the *ajimez* (double windows with central pillar). Christian architecture in the West was also influenced by the simple dome constructions in the *mihrab* tract, with the octagon created by corner niches and intersecting binding arches (plate 4).

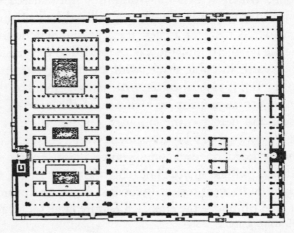

3. The ground plan of the Great Mosque in Cordova reproduced here shows the different extensions, the first two setting back the *mihrab* laid on the central axis. The third extension under al-Mansur could not be carried out in the same direction because the terrain slopes down to the river, but had to be done to one side. This involved re-planning the courtyard to correspond to the new width of the sanctuary.

The fortress-like character of the strongly buttressed outer walls in most of the buildings so far mentioned is clearly reminiscent of the earlier garrison mosques. Regional peculiarities are manifest in the ground plan: in Egypt it approximated to a square, whereas in Syria a horizontal rectangle and in the Mahgreb a vertical rectangle was the rule. One plan which was to be of considerable importance falls, however, right outside the general scheme; this is the Dome of the Rock, the Qubbat as-Sakhra (the so-called Mosque of ʿOmar) in Jerusalem. It is in the form of an octagon, the exterior articulated by ogival arcading and salient porches; inside it has one octagonal and one concentric, circular ring of supports above which rises the double wooden dome on a drum (plate 5). This unusual arrangement arose from the need to build round the holy rock; a contributing factor may have been the desire to place an equally imposing monument beside the Christian rotunda, the Church of the Ascension, at the same place. Moreover, the Caliph 'Abd al-Malik began the Qubbat as-Sakhra in 691 with the express intention of creating a pilgrimage sanctuary on the site of the temples of Solomon and Herod, to compete with the sanctuary built round another holy stone, the Ka'ba in Mecca. This latter monument, with its peculiar pre-Islamic cult significance and its special ritual cannot be reckoned as a true mosque; nor did it receive its present form until later.

Castles, Palaces and Fortresses

We know nothing of the appearance of the ancient Umayyad residence at Damascus, and even had it been preserved it would not have sufficed to give us a picture of the courts of the Caliphs. These were held to a great extent outside the capital, from which the princes were for ever fleeing to the deserts in which they trusted. There they had grown up, and many of them spent the greater part of their lives in the garrison palaces (hira) and pleasure castles (badiya) which they built in the wastes eastwards from the Jordan and in the Syrian desert, at places where in the rainy season tiny streams made a little vegetation possible. The ruins of many such seats are known. Materials must have been brought from afar, and the murderous climate and perpetual shortage of water must have claimed many a victim before they were brought to completion. Two relatively well-preserved examples illustrate particularly clearly the two main types of these desert castles: Mshatta and Qusayr 'Amra. The latter, first discovered by Musil in 1898, served the Caliph al-Walid as a hunting lodge and baths. Its hall with triple tunnel vaults springing almost from the ground can be seen as the translation into stone of Mesopotamian brick building. It comprised a main hall with a niche, and smaller rooms with provision for the bath; the water was brought from a well on to the roof and led from there into the bathrooms. The floors were paved with marble and mosaic, and the upper walls were decorated with paintings which provide the chief charm of this *badiya* (see below).

Mshatta (i.e. winter camp) on the other hand exemplifies the larger type of desert palace which arose from the fortified nomad encampment (*hira*), with influences from the Roman frontier fort

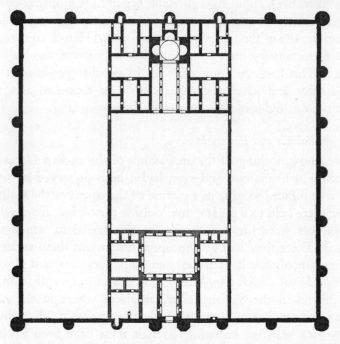

4. The only part of the Desert Castle of Mshatta that was virtually completed was the residence complex set in the rear section of the central tract, which was divided into three; the buildings at the front with the mosque were only begun, but the grouping is clear. The empty tracts to each side were also to be built on, and have given rise to hypothetical reconstructions (*inter alia* by Schulz, Creswell).

(fig 4). An outer wall 144 metres square, flanked with round towers, encloses the building, of which not even the central tract was completed. It consists of an entrance block with gatehouse, courtyard and lateral rooms, a large court of honour with a central water basin, and the residence proper. This comprises a central three-aisled basilical hall terminating in a triple-apsed dome chamber, and dwelling rooms symmetrically arranged on either side. The spaces on each side of the central tract were intended to be built over as well; as it was, they must have served simply for the tents of the troops and following of the Caliph. The gigantic complex has only one entrance, on either side of which the façade (now in the Berlin Islamic Museum) was richly decorated with sculpture (see below). Some insignificant fragments of figurative sculpture were found in the court.

It is generally assumed that Mshatta is indebted to Persian models, and indeed the plan has much in common with the famous Sasanid palaces. On the other hand—above all in the triconchos of the throne room—Byzantine influence is unmistakable. That it is to be dated to the Islamic period has sometimes been questioned, but this dating is supported *inter alia* by the presence of a hall which can only be explained as a mosque, with a recessed niche in the southern wall (to the right of the entrance). At all events we can presume—and, in the ultimate analysis, this is the overriding factor—that the layout was similar in the camp palaces of the Lakhmids and Ghassanids. These were Arab tribes who had advanced into Mesopotamia and Syria in the pre-Islamic period; thus there was already a national tradition established. It was to remain important in the following phase, under the Abbasids.

Other desert castles besides Mshatta have been excavated in recent decades, all related in plan, although each has its peculiarities. North-east of Damascus, towards the Euphrates, are two sites at Qasr al-Hair. The western site, al-Gharbi, has a gateway between round towers, with blind arcading and battlements, a square court with columns, groups of rooms on two floors and doorways with ornamental pierced lattices; the court has now been re-erected very correctly in the Damascus Museum. The eastern fort (ash-Sharqi) consists of two fortified enclosures with semi-circular towers; the smaller enclosure, much damaged, has an imposing gateway; the larger has the remains of a mosque, arcading of very slightly pointed arches and an inscription about the Caliph Hisham dated 110 H (A.D. 728-729) on one pillar. Between the two stands a four-cornered minaret. Two further ruins, Rusafa and Jabal Sais, have only been superficially examined.

Khirbat al-Minya near Tabgha on Lake Galilee was shown by

excavations carried out between 1932 and 1939 to be a small two-storeyed Umayyad *badiya* and not, as had been previously thought, a Roman fort. It is exceptional in being sited, not in the desert steppe but in fertile and delightful country. It has a massive gate house, a mosque, and five-part and other groups of rooms round the pillared court, some with fine mosaic floors (fig 5). Lastly

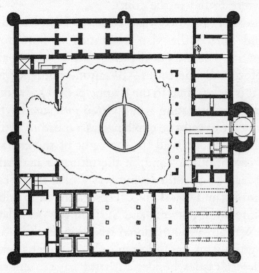

5. Excavation of the Castle of Khirbat al-Minya near Tabgha on the Lake of Galilee was begun in 1932 by the Görres-Gesellschaft, and later continued in conjunction with the Islamic Section of the Berlin Museum, but it was stopped in 1939. It has a two storeyed lay-out round a pillared courtyard, with mosque, throne room and several groups of rooms. Some rooms had mosaic floors: for others the material was still to hand in a workshop. The structure, probably built under Walid I (705–715), has recently been re-examined. Cf. *Palästina-Hefte, Deutsches Verein vom Heiligen Lande*, 1939, Heft 17–20.

Khirbat al-Mafjar at Jericho, near the Dead Sea, formed a stately complex with entrance hall, pillared court, upper storey, mosque with a tower above the *mihrab*, an underground, cooled living apartment (*sirdab*) and a monumental bath house. It was fitted out with stone and stucco decoration, the latter mostly figurative, mosaics and paintings of which only fragments remain. The whole site was published in detail in 1959 by R. W. Hamilton, who attributes its foundation to al-Walid II (murdered in 744).

No traces remain of the earliest residences in Egypt and North Africa, nor is much to be learnt from the formless ruins which are all that remain of the Caliphs' palace of Cordova, begun in 784 and frequently enlarged until the 10th century. The inexact descriptions of Arab authors have little to add to our picture. Excavations in Madinat az-Zahra fill the gap to some extent, but very imperfectly as yet. They laid bare parts of the residence of 'Abd ar-Rahman III, once so lavishly praised, which was built in

6. The Ribat of Susa was laid out in 771, and the watch tower built in 821, which gave it its final form; but it lost its military importance by the end of the 9th century. (After a drawing by G. Marçais, *Manuel d'art musulman*, p. 48. Studied in detail by A. Lézine, *Le ribat de Sousse*, 1956.)

936 before the gates of the capital against a cliff, rising in terraces against the hillside. So far at any rate they have not provided a reliable reconstruction of the plan, but it has been established that the often very extensive living quarters were fitted out in the same style as the large mosque.

The main defence of Islam in North Africa, both against attacks by sea from the Christian countries and on land from the rebellious Berbers, was vested in the *ribat*, the strongholds of monastic knights. They almost all arose in the 8th and 9th centuries, and were built close together, particularly on the Tunisian coast, though now most of them have vanished without trace. However, two of them are sufficiently well preserved to enable their original appearance to be reconstructed with some confidence. The *ribat* of Susa acquired special importance as the base for equipping expeditions to attack Sicily. A defensive wall enclosed a rectangular site comprising living cells, ablution rooms, an eleven-aisled flat-roofed sanctuary with a dome over the *mihrab*, and a cylindrical minaret which served equally for the call to prayer and as a signalling tower (fig 6). The *ribat* of Monastir was similar in plan, but had in addition a graveyard between the *qibla* and the fortification wall. These military monasteries were also built along the Moroccan coast, and in the Sahara they formed bases for the propagation of Islam into the interior of Africa. From these arose the 'Almoravid' movement (*al-murabitin*, i.e. Ribat monk) which changed the course of events in the Mahgreb at the end of the 11th century.

Umayyad Architectural Decoration

In nearly all the mosques of the first period much use was made of materials from earlier buildings. These materials were not only those available locally, but were transported from afar. Byzantine columns and capitals were particularly prized. This practice went on even as late as the first extensions to Cordova, where they did not evolve their own type of capital until the late 10th century. At first the walls were faced with marble and stone inlay, for example in Damascus and Jerusalem, and this probably did not deviate far from Late Antique patterns. The mosaic decoration in the Dome of the Rock and in the courtyard of the Umayyad mosque in Damascus is laid in novel compositions which are most effectively adapted to the Islamic context; but even they cannot give more than an approximate idea of an 'Early Islamic style' of ornament, since it was executed by craftsmen schooled in Byzantium (plate 9). Greek craftsmen were still being sent for to Cordova in the 10th century to furnish the *mihrab* wall and the dome chambers in front of it with mosaic, and though in fact they worked in the prescribed style, we cannot accept their designs either with complete conviction as typical of Umayyad art. Indeed the paintings at Qusayr 'Amra are strongly Hellenistic, both as to composition and in the treatment of the individual motifs. It is true that beside hunting, bathing and genre scenes, representations of the zodiac and of the ages of man there is also the figure of the reigning Caliph opposed to the foes of Islam, but this does not alter the fact that they belong entirely to the previous period and underwent hardly any development at all in the new one. Again, Sasanid influence is unmistakable on the paintings which have survived in a few rooms of Qasr al Hair-al-Gharbi.

A study of the development of ornament in the first phase of Islamic art is best begun with the façade of Mshatta. It is strongly articulated by an acanthus frieze broken up into a zigzag with balancing large rosettes, and the ground is then further broken up with fine carving into a large number of motifs. These are picked out in deeply undercut relief which makes great play of light and shade. The façade to the left of the gateway has a preponderance of animal figures between vines or in scrolls (plate 6), whereas the right-hand side, obviously of later date, has nothing but plant scrolls, as though the patron suddenly took religious umbrage at the representation of animate beings and gave the order to change the motifs. The uncertainty of the stone carvers is clearly expressed in the different attempts to give unity of composition to the mass of tendrils in the triangles (plate 7). In their spasmodic efforts to give ornamental stylization to the luxuriously rampant and still naturalistic leaf and scroll work we can witness the birth pangs of the arabesque. The marble panels of the *mihrab* at Cordova show this motif when it has reached its full deployment (plate 8). It now covers its appointed surface in a sure and elegant pattern, accommodating itself happily to every attempt to organize it into new forms. Between the two carvings lies the whole development of Umayyad style, and a span of two centuries, and yet the attitude to surface filling and the light-and-shadow effect of deep relief have remained the same. These two principles dominated the treatment of capitals as well, which endeavoured more or less consistently to adapt the acanthus tradition to the new style.

The stucco decoration found both in the Khirbat Mafjar and Qasr al-Hair (the latter now in the Museum at Damascus) presents an extraordinary wealth of abstract and figurative motifs, for the most part inspired by Iranian models, but straightway developed in conformity with the new style. We have an indication of the appearance of the earliest prayer niches from a *mihrab* which was discovered in a small sanctuary of later date in Baghdad and was probably brought from Syria by the Caliph Mansur for his first, still very modest mosque (fig 7). It is made from a single block of

7. E. Herzfeld (*Archäologische Reise im Euphrat- und Tigris-gebiet*, 1920, II, pp. 139 ff) recognized the monolithic marble niche in the Jami al-Khasaki in Baghdad as the *mihrab* probably brought by Mansur, the founder of Baghdad, from Syria and set up in his mosque in the Round City (now in the Baghdad Museum).

marble with a lovely conch upheld by engaged columns, and a central ornamental band. The association with the approximately contemporary façade of Mshatta is clearly apparent. In Cordova the niche is much more imposing, constructed as an eight-sided chapel with blind arcading, but it is roofed over with a very similar monolithic marble shell. The extravagant elaboration of the *mihrab* area of al-Hakam extended to the cusped arches, in which smooth and richly decorated faces alternate, so that the impression created by alternation of colour which pervades the whole mosque takes on special ceremonial emphasis in the proximity of the niche.

According to the reports of Arab authors figurative sculpture in the round seems to have been used in the designs for Madinat az-Zahra. From there, too, come several of the peculiar rectangular marble ablution basins which have also been found on other Spanish sites, decorated in close reference to the decoration on the building. The plant motifs are still completely in the style of the Umayyad mosque, while the eagles attacking gazelles of early oriental derivation which are usual on the narrow sides are somewhat surprising in view of the ritual intention of the object (plate 11b). The basins are nearly all closely dated by inscriptions.

If the wooden members of buildings had been preserved in greater quantity we would have more information about Umayyad decoration. The beams in Qairawan were renewed in Fatimid times, and only recently have parts of the earlier ceiling painting been uncovered from beneath the later vaulting of the Great Mosque in Cordova.

The decadence of the epoch in Spain, which set in with the political decline of the Caliphate, is most clearly shown in the recently restored remains of the 11th century stucco arches of the Aljaferia, the ruler's castle at Sargossa. The disturbing proliferation and combination of ornamental and architectonic forms gives drastic expression to the cloying effect of an art which is clearly no longer viable. The only exception was in the strict canon observed by calligraphic decoration. Without any noticeable provincial variations the luxuriant Kufic hand (so-called from the early Islamic centre of culture in Iraq) was adhered to and continued for decade after decade on building inscriptions and grave stones.

Umayyad Minor Arts

The most important item of mosque furniture was the pulpit (*minbar*) which stood beside the prayer niche and very soon received the characteristic form it was to retain during its further development: two triangular panels of wood with narrow steps between, a parapet and an entrance door, and later a baldaquin-like roof. The earliest example of this kind stands in Sidi 'Oqba. It was not in fact made until the 9th century, during the Abbasid period, when it was commissioned in Baghdad for dedication in Qairawan, but stylistically its carving places it unmistakably in the Umayyad period. Apart from a few panels with plant motifs reminiscent of Mshatta the individual fields surrounded by scroll work have geometric patterns; these show a quite astonishing sensitivity (plate 10). The variety of basketry and interlacery, of knots and lattice patterns so imaginatively combined puts into the shade all other work that we know from the Migration period which was, quite apart from this example, the most fertile period for this kind of work. Perhaps there were artists from northern Mesopotamia at work here, for in Diyarbakr some pre-Islamic pillar shafts survive which are decorated with related designs.

Very little else remains from this early period in the way of mosque furniture, apart from a number of copies of the Koran, which were at that time written almost exclusively on parchment in horizontal format, in lapidary Kufic script. Borders and chapter heads etc were embellished in gold and a few colours (plate 12b). The earliest bindings suggest Coptic models. They are of leather, with very simple geometric designs in blind tooling.

Let us now turn to secular furniture. The treatment of mosque basins already discussed is related to that of the numerous surviving chests and boxes of ivory, which in the 10th century were the glory of the carvers' guilds of Cordova and Madinat az-Zahra. Their beginnings can be found in the pyxes and smaller bone carvings of the 8th century which are still clearly related to Mshatta and are presumably of Syrian origin; from there the technique came to the Western capital. The lids of the cylindrical boxes are usually domed, those of the rectangular chests flat or roof shaped; and there is a wide variety of sizes. In the true Umayyad style of surface treatment the whole body of the object is covered with close, often quite deeply carved decoration. Besides the pure plant decoration and animals over leaf and scroll work, there are round medallions with figured scenes: revellers, musicians,

enthroned monarchs with servants, falconers on horseback, etc
(plate 12a). Kufic inscriptions round the border frequently name
the giver of the commission, always a member of the Umayyad
court, and the date of manufacture. A later group, made no longer
in Cordova itself but in Cuenca in the 11th century, has poorer
decoration, flatter and more formal (plate 11a). These pieces were
much coveted in the Christian West as jewel caskets, and were
particularly popular as presents at royal weddings.

Eagles attacking gazelles, roundels of animals and other motifs
used in Cordovan carving are found again on multi-coloured
textiles; these by technical analogy with later, unquestionably
Moorish textiles would be attributable without further evidence
to Spain. They represent the earliest surviving products of the
Andalusian silk industry which flourished in the Umayyad period.
Its foundation is due once again to the activity of Syrian Arabs
in Spain. It is probable that as early as the 10th century a government manufacture (tiraz) was set up to provide the court with
silk cloths. This followed the highly perfected pattern of the
Egyptian organizations (vide p. 74).

A cast bronze figure of a stag found in Madinat az-Zahra, now
in the Museum of Cordova, and a chest of chased silver-gilt dated
to 975 in the cathedral at Gerona are interesting as examples of
metal craft; in ceramics we know mainly of faiences with green
and manganese brown painting on a white glaze with simple,
sometimes animate motifs.

CHAPTER TWO

Art under the Abbasids

WHEN the Islamic West finally broke away from the Abbasid Caliphate and the eastern capital was moved eastwards from Damascus to Baghdad, newly founded near the ancient Persian city of Ktesiphon, the transfer affected all aspects of culture, including art. The Persian element increased in importance in the Orient alongside the Arab. The bond with Hellenistic antiquity formed in the first phase of Muslim civilization was loosened, and new ties were formed with the Sasanid tradition still flourishing in Mesopotamia. The process was furthered by the many Persian nobles who reached great power and influence at the court. As the Caliphs gradually sensed the danger they were in of being completely Persianized, even in the political sphere, they tried to combat it by surrounding themselves with Turkish guards and favouring the tractable Turanian provinces. This only resulted in further undermining the original and traditional hegemony of the Arab element, which consequently became increasingly unreliable.

On the Persian side national aspirations were bound to grow, encouraged by the protecting wing of their religious sect, the Shi'a. Powerful personalities in the leadership brought about virtual separation from the central power. Under the dynasties that arose—Saffarids, Tahirids, Samanids, Buyids and others—rich patrons fostered the memory of the country's great past and thus ensured a second flowering of art in the Sasanid tradition, which in many ways conflicted with the cultural influence of Baghdad. The new, Turkish-inspired style of the Caliphs only filtered sporadically into Persia, while Ibn Tulun was carrying it to Egypt and others spread it as far as Turkestan.

Meanwhile the fate of the Caliphate was sealed as the Turkish element grew stronger. There was indeed a spell of Persian dominance towards the end of the 9th century during the military dictatorship of the Buyids, but Seljuk princes succeeded at last in wresting all the power to themselves, and Baghdad itself when it was conquered by the Mongols in 1256 was already virtually a Seljuk city.

Hardly a trace remains of the oriental residence in the time of its greatest splendour under Harun ar-Rashid and his successors. Its loss is all the more disappointing since it formed the backcloth to a world-famous cycle of fairy tales. When the Caliph Mansur (762–766) created the new capital on the Tigris he tried an experiment in town planning, interesting though not the first of its kind, and built the city to a circular plan, surrounded by a main wall with round towers and an outer wall. Four narrow long gate houses, joined by an outer and an inner ring road, divided the residential area into quadrants, each of which had eight to twelve radial lanes; towards the centre the building blocks opened into arcades. In the centre the palace and chief mosque stood in isolation (fig 8). The same Mansur repeated his experiment with the circular town when he laid out a new town of horseshoe shape on the Euphrates near the ancient site of Raqqa. Harun ar-Rashid resided there between 796 and 808. Its mud walls, fortified with towers, have survived, but only as shapeless ruins.

More important was the foundation of Samarra above Baghdad on the Tigris, which served as a residence for the Abbasids for half a century (838–883). It demands consideration as one of the most magnificent urban creations of all time. It extended for 33 kilometres along the river, and anything in any way connected with the court was concentrated here. The scattered ruins were excavated in great part by E. Herzfeld between 1911 and 1913. They have yielded invaluable evidence of the artistic activity of the Abbasids, otherwise very sparsely preserved. The layout of streets and drains, mosques, palaces and private houses, some impressively extensive, have been brought to light, and the objects

4

found among them compensate in some degree for the total loss of ancient Baghdad.

The direct cause of the departure to Samarra was the growing friction between Arab and Turkish troops, and the unpopularity of the latter with the populace, which had little contact with the Caliph himself. He thought himself safer away from the capital,

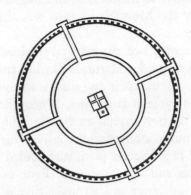

8. From the very detailed reports of the Arab authors, which even gave the street names, E. Herzfeld (*Archäologische Reise* II, fig 180) was able to reconstruct the plan of the Round City quite clearly. The sketch given here shows the basic scheme. The original site has entirely disappeared and has been built over, so that it cannot be excavated.

but soon came completely under the power of his Turkish praetorian guard, by whom many of his successors were deposed or murdered, so that the return to Baghdad in 883 is to be regarded as an act of self-assertion by the Abbasids.

Mosques

The form of the mosque remained as it had already developed —an open court surrounded by pillared halls, deepened on the side of the *qibla* into a sanctuary. The great mosque of Mansur was still built of mud brick, with columns and capitals of wood; it was given a new surrounding wall of baked brick by Harun. It has disappeared without trace, but for the marble *mihrab*, carved from a single block and still entirely in Umayyad style (see above). Subsequently, the primacy of Mesopotamia brought about a substantial change, for the use of baked bricks was now universally adopted, and monolithic columns were no longer used, but piers of laid brick, usually with engaged corner columns, on which pointed or ogival arches were always laid. With few exceptions the rows of piers run parallel to the *qibla* wall, contrary to the usual plan of the pillared mosques, and a logical consequence was that the *mihrab* aisle was no longer broadened or roofed over with a dome, and the transeptal meaning was lost. The tower now usually stood free outside the rectangle of the wall.

The most imposing site of the period by reason of its outer measurements was the great mosque of Mutawakkil in Samarra (846–852), the sides of its rectangle measuring 260 and 180 metres and providing space for more than 100,000 worshippers. The flat roof apparently rested without arches directly on the octagonal piers with their engaged marble columns. The surrounding wall strengthened with round towers is still reminiscent of the garrison mosques; outside this wall the *malwiye* stands isolated: a spiral-shaped tower with outer ramp whose origin has been sought both in the Babylonian stepped tower (*ziggurat*) and in Chinese buildings of the T'ang period (plate 13a). A second mosque in Samarra, Abu Dulaf, is somewhat smaller, with a similar tower, badly preserved, and a closely related ground plan, but with its roof resting on pointed arches; these, exceptionally, run perpendicular to the *qibla* wall. We have no adequate records of similar mosques in Baghdad itself; all we know of one built in 785 in the Rusafa district of the town is that it had two courtyards. For the great Persian mosques of this period we are unfortunately thrown al most entirely on to speculations based on literary sources, or later radical alterations. The crumbled ruin of the old mosque in Shiraz of 871 shows that there were pillars of baked brick in the *haram* (prayer hall) with pointed arches and raftered roof, and these supports seem also to have been used in the ancient Friday mosque in Isfahan (760–762) which, exceptionally, had its minaret rising over the *qibla* wall; its present form is very much changed. Smaller cult buildings in Iran very early took on a national character, to some extent with Sasanid reminiscences. At the mosque in Damghan the pointed arches rest without capitals on short very squat pillars of brick. So-called kiosk mosques are a special variant, simply a rather deep vaulted hall of brick, sometimes with a dome chamber attached. In Turkestan the courtyard plan with pillared hall persisted especially long; Merv in the year 1000 possessed no less than three chief or Friday mosques.

The imposing and well-preserved mosque which Ahmed Ibn Tulun built in his garrison town al-Qatai' (in Old Cairo) in 877–879 kept very close to the Samarra type. The prayer hall has pointed arches on five rows of brick piers with engaged pillars which are also of baked brick, plastered with stucco; the spandrels are lightened by windows. The heavy pointed arch which is dominant here seems to have made an impression in the West; when it appears in romanesque churches it usually has the Tulunid outline. The completely flat roof makes a peculiar contrast to the upward swing of the arch (plate 13b, 14). The fortress-like character of the building has gone, and the outer façade is articulated by round niches and windows, and is crowned with elaborate cresting. The minaret here stands outside, but the spiral with its outer ramp continues from a square base with inside steps.

Palaces and Private Houses

To this day on the site of the ancient Ktesiphon by the Tigris stand the ruins of the one-time Sasanid residence with a gigantic vaulted hall (*iwan*).* In early Islamic times the building must have been in good repair and could not have failed to impress the Abbasid architects. Their main borrowing was the *iwan* which from now on played a leading part in their designs. Another influence still at work on the planning of the sovereign's residence was the camp palace of the Lakhmids, al-Hira (see above p. 39), now, alas, vanished without trace.

These influences can be clearly recognized at two imposing sites: Ukhaydir and Balkuwara. The former lies 40 kilometres WSW of the famous pilgrimage centre of Kerbela. It was founded perhaps in the 9th century as the residence of Qarmatian leaders, whose power rested primarily on rebellious sectarians and Arab

* The *iwan* is a vaulted niche, often very large, closed on three sides and open on the fourth.

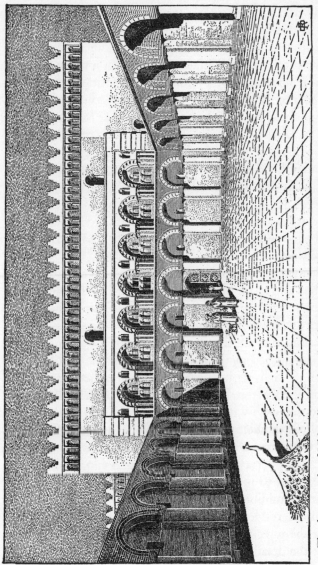

9. The desert castle of Ukhaydir was described by G. Bell and O. Reuther. It is not yet known who built it. It is unlikely that it was the Qarmatians; they caused much trouble to the Abbasids and were important politically in the late 9th century, but they would hardly be concerned with such a representative building, being a sect organized on communist lines, and besides, they had their centre of power further south in Ahsa after about 900. The palace was completed and parts of it are well preserved, so that reconstructions, such as that reproduced here (by O. Reuther, Ochestr, Leipzig, 1912) can be relied upon.

tribes, among them some Bedouins who had penetrated into Iraq. Ukhaydir was a palace complex fortified with towers and girded round with another strong wall with four gates, though the palace itself was only to be entered through one portal. The ground plan shows an entrance hall, court of honour and audience hall as in the central tract at Mshatta, though on a more modest scale, and also makes clear the symmetrical disposition of the living quarters to each side round a further four courtyards. The mosque, recognizable by its *mihrab* recess, lay as at Mshatta to the right of the entrance. Ukhaydir is mainly built of rough slab masonry, though brick was retained for the vaulting, and it has both round and pointed arches which were also used purely decoratively as arcading along the walls. Probably Mansur's 'Golden Castle' inside the Round City was laid out in a similar manner. It had a court of honour, an *iwan*, throne room and upper dome room (with the famous Green Dome which collapsed in 941).

It is expressly reported of the castle of Balkuwara at Samarra that it was planned on the model of *al-Nira* (fig 10). The Caliph Mutawakkil had the castle built by his son Mu'tazz between 854 and 859. Here several large courtyards follow one behind the other; the core of the layout, which stretches for over a kilometre in either direction, is again the court of honour and a number of throne rooms, arranged in the form of a cross, which continue lengthwise as open halls with frontages of three arches. Right and left of this central tract stretch the porticoes (*riwaq*) of the dozen or so dwelling houses, each with its own courtyard, and towards the Tigris out beyond the belt of walls the plan is finished off with a garden with water basin and a harbour for boats. The citadel dominating the western bank, the Qasr al-'Ashiq, enclosed a smaller palace, built to much the same plan, in 880, right at the end of Samarra's building period.

At the Caliph's residence itself (*al-Jausaq*) one high gate hall still soars over the wreckage; here again the general arrangement was the same; the details of the ground plan revealed by excavation still await publication. Even the dwelling houses, though always of one storey, were often very large; they sometimes comprised fifty rooms, all built to the same plan, generally of unbaked

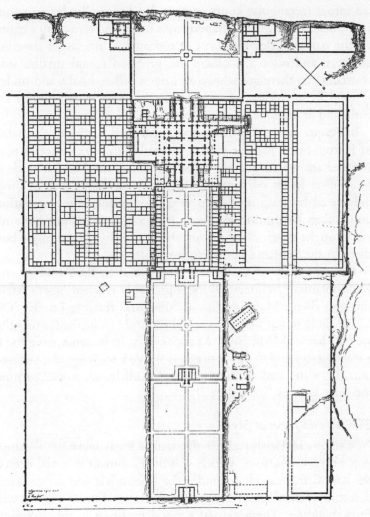

10. The ground plan of Balkuwara shown here is taken from a survey on the site by E. Herzfeld (*Erster vorläufiger Bericht über die Ausgrabungen von Samarra*, Berlin, 1912, pp. 32 ff). The mosque here lay isolated to the right of the second forecourt, turned away towards the *qibla*.

mud brick, as in the wing blocks at Balkuwara. A covered entrance led into a rectangular court surrounded by smaller living rooms and offices, and with a T-shaped main room and two corner rooms on the narrow side. This type is repeated in the larger dwelling quarters, and often the offices are grouped round smaller side-courts. Then there are sometimes open pillared halls and underground living rooms (*sirdab*) for the hot season. All houses had baths and drainage.

In Raqqa on the Euphrates there still lie the ruins of the palace of Harun, but it has not yet been possible to reconstruct its plan. Neither are we adequately informed about the Meidan castle of Ibn Tulun in his garrison town, which probably was as much influenced by Iraqi models as was his mosque. The excavations undertaken by the Metropolitan Museum in Nishapur have not yet brought much clarification about the dwelling houses built there in the Samanid period (9th century).

The Aghlabids of Qairawan were allied to the Abbasids, and Mesopotamian architectural ideas probably reached North Africa through them. Many of the architectural features on the 'Old Castle' built in 801 near the capital certainly came thence together with its name al-'Abbasiya. As at Samarra, its presence gave rise to a stately city. In 876 the court was moved to Raqqada, where a gigantic water tank with heavy walls still stands to call to mind the once famous 'Sea palace'.

The Abbasid Imperial Style

Whereas in Umayyad art decorative ideas were for the most part expressed in stone, which was the dominant material even in the later Cordovan phase, under the Abbasids it was stucco which determined the form of decoration, because of its association with brick building. There existed a good tradition in this technique from the Sasanid period, and all that was needed was to re-form the repertoire of motifs. In Samarra all the living rooms were furnished with stucco dadoes, above which the walls were then divided up into alcoves of various shapes (plate 15), or decorated with paintings. Probably the same thing was usual earlier in Baghdad. The oldest examples discovered by excavation show in various forms a rather stylized but still somewhat naturalistically conceived decoration of vine leaves, grapes etc, which is still definitely reminiscent of Mshatta in the whole method of covering the surface and in the light and shade effect of the deeply carved relief. In the following phases these and other plant motifs are visibly more schematized, until they deteriorate into a totally denaturalized bevelled style with repeat patterns.

This bevelled style is the artistic contribution of Samarra; it signifies no less than a complete ornamental revolution and the establishment of an individual Abbasid style of decoration, with Turkish contribution. For there can be no doubt that it was the spirit of the Scythian animal style still alive in Turanian folk art that here stood sponsor; it was, clearly, taken over from metal craft and wood carving and was used mainly on the weapons, saddlery and ornaments reaching Mesopotamia in the train of the mercenaries attaching themselves to the Caliph. Perhaps one or other of the Turkish generals was interested in introducing the methods of decoration prevalent in his homeland; and the Caliph, feeling himself more and more dependent on his Turkish guards now he was in Samarra, will have been the more easily influenced. At any rate the bevelled, or slant, carving is so exclusively characteristic of Scythian nomad art that there is virtually no question of any other origin. The number of the schematized motifs is in itself surprisingly small, though they were subject to manifold variations; it was the custom to treat them in textile fashion, aligned in continuous rows along the dado. The door-posts are then always distinguished with their own design, and show particularly clearly the tendency to reproduce wood carving. Patterns were no longer carved into the plaster, but were pressed on with moulds, making the work of decoration more rapid.

The same style was of course used in Samarra on woodwork, to which it was best suited, and also on occasion on marble, and it spread elsewhere in Mesopotamia, where it is met chiefly on alabaster capitals. Ibn Tulun, himself a Turk and perhaps feeling a native affinity with the new style, took it direct from Samarra to Egypt, where it can be seen at its most effective in the framing bands of stucco on the walls, arches and windows of his mosque (plate 14), as well as on its wooden soffits. It is likely that the figured wood reliefs which, according to Arab authors, decorated his palace, were inspired by it too.

The splendid collection of carved ornamental panels from private houses which have survived from the Tulunid period show how far this Abbasid fashion became general in Fostat. It can even be recognized in the designs on silk and jewellery. It is not surprising that it also penetrated the Christian monuments of this time in Egypt: in one of the monasteries in Wadi Natrun, Deir es-Suriani, the walls, mouldings of the arches and bands of decoration were all embellished in about 900 entirely in this style, with some original development of individual motifs apart from the cross symbol. In Persia on the other hand there are only a few isolated monuments, such as the mosque of Nayin (late 10th century) which adopted Abbasid stucco decoration, often applying it in a highly individual way; but it seems also to have reached as far as eastern Iran in dwelling houses, as is proved by the excavations at Nishapur, and in Turkestan it may in places have survived into the Seljuk period.

Decorative inscriptions, surprisingly, have not been found in Samarra, and we have to turn to examples outside Iraq. In epigraphy Kufic was still prevalent, and no longer with the hieratic stiffness of the Umayyad period, but already tending to more graceful forms. Many copies of the Koran are known from this time in which the border medallions are done in the bevelled style.

The Ceramics of Samarra

The excavation of Samarra added a great deal to our knowledge of early Islamic pottery, besides producing the other small finds, such as glass objects of very varied and extremely refined technique. The luxury wares used there were in part native products, and in part imports from eastern Asia. As regards these latter, we have here the first indubitable evidence that Chinese white porcelain and so-called celadon were not only being produced but exported in the 9th century. T'ang stoneware with splashed glazes was also found and other pieces show that the Islamic potters were endeavouring to produce a similar ware.

Their own most magnificent achievement however lay in another direction: they invented lustre painting, a method of applying a metallic sheen to glazed faience to remarkably splendid effect. This technique they used on vessels and wall tiles in such a way that several tones of lustre showed side by side. At this time tiles were usually made square in shape and were used as a decorative facing on palaces and mosques. The *mihrab* of the mosque in Qairawan is laid with tiles whose provenance from Baghdad is expressly proven. Lustre vessels must have been particularly welcome as substitutes for the pure gold utensils forbidden by the Koran. They were evidently sent all over the Muslim world, for fragments of unmistakable Iraqi lustre ware have been found in Spain (Madinat az-Zahra), in Egypt (Fostat) and above all in Persia, where whole vessels have occurred in great quantity. Sooner or later in these three countries, as in Syria, the production of their own lustre ware began (in Egypt it started under the Tulunids). The motifs are independent of those evolved in stucco decoration: stylized animal and human figures, good luck inscriptions and certain devices typical of ceramics come into their own (plate 16a).

Samarra also revealed examples of other ceramic skills beside the lustre wares, among which the cobalt blue painting on a creamy white ground is deserving of special attention, because like lustre technique it was carried into other Islamic countries and practised there for centuries. Both types are included in the term Samarra ware, although they are probably less to be regarded as local products than as acquired from the potters' guilds of Baghdad. Neither kilns nor wasters have so far been found in Samarra.

Survival of Sasanid Art

Art production in other spheres was still carried on in a decidedly decadent Sasanid style, both in Mesopotamia and in Persia. The wall paintings that have survived in the palace at Samarra are unfortunately no more than fragmentary. But they are enough to show a difference from Qusay 'Amra. There are no pictorial compositions, only purely decorative themes (dancing girls, huntresses, animals in combat etc), and in almost all of them their Sasanid ancestry is apparent (plate 16b). Exceptionally, Persian patterns such as the wing palmette intruded here even into the stucco decoration, and outside the Caliph's court we meet large decorative medallions of the same material which still use nothing but animals and abstract patterns in a characteristically pre-Islamic style, although they can hardly have been much earlier than the Samarra art which belongs entirely to the new world. In the pottery even Parthian traditions live on here and there without noticeable change, long into the Abbasid period.

These manifestations at Samarra may be no more than chance remnants of an irrevocably past era, but at the courts of the Persian princes, who ultimately seceded quite consciously from Baghdad, it became deliberate policy to cherish the artistic traditions of early Iran, just as in literature the threat of Arabization was being met with a cultivation of the native language. For several centuries to come sets of silver ware were produced with representations of Persian kings, exactly in the style of the famous Sasanid dishes, and in West Turkestan and Khorasan, within the Samanid sphere of influence, bronze casting was maintained at a high artistic level in the production of large table ware. We thus possess a large number of pieces of metal work which are very difficult to date. They retain pre-Islamic motifs, but misunderstood details betray them as works of decadence. How gradual was the process of Islamization here can be seen by the ewers and jugs of the 8th to 10th centuries, which seem to be conceived entirely in archaic style. The first attempts to decorate the body of the vessel with copper inlay were made at this time, leading to the splendid inlaid technique of the 11th and 12th centuries.

Things were little different in textiles. The silk industry of the Sasanids, splendid specimens of which lie in our early church treasures, continued into the new era and was only gradually Islamized. True, the repertoire of motifs was extended beyond the usual lions' combat, winged horses, etc, but the new subjects were often not understood and were arranged much more clumsily and more schematically. Thus we have textiles of late Sasanid style right into the 11th century, apparently produced both in western and eastern Persia, which testify to the undiminished skill of the weavers (plates 17a and 17b).

Conservative tendencies were also at work in native ceramics, which is more difficult to understand since the new processes invented in Iraq with all their revolutionary implications can not easily have been ignored in Iran. Yet the Iranians contented themselves with importing lustre wares from Baghdad, and themselves went on producing, chiefly in Buyid territory in western and northern Persia, rougher faiences with scratched decoration (Gabri ware). They preferred Sasanid horsemen or animal figures in stiff hieratic style, and only gradually adopted the more fluent Islamic type of abstract ornament; sometimes they even show unmistakable references to the earlier metal style. Other potters, particularly in Nishapur, concentrated on strong colour effects, and it is evident that here folk art was being played against court art. Samarqand came to the fore in the 9th century as a ceramic centre with a very elegant ware with finely balanced calligraphic ornament, dark brown on a creamy-white ground.

Lastly as to architecture: the strong influence in Persia was the feeling in favour of the old principles of construction and certain types of building of Iranian origin such as the tower mausoleum; the Seljuks took up these traditions and interpreted them in a monumental fashion suited to the character of the art of the following epoch.

MEDIAEVAL ISLAMIC ART

CHAPTER THREE

The Fatimid Style

THE Caliphate of Baghdad suffered one of its most serious blows when in 969 the Fatimids, who had seized power in North Africa, advanced to Egypt and gave it political and cultural independence. They were Berbers by nationality, and founded their new city of Cairo with a concept of art which they had learnt in their homeland, based on Umayyad-Moorish work. They were, moreover, Shi'ites in religion and so open to influences from Persia where the same beliefs held sway. Thus their activity was fed from both sides as well as from local tradition, from the West only in the beginning, but constantly renewed from Persia. The arts benefited above all from the freer interpretation of the ban on representing living creatures. Added to this were lively connections with the Christian West, for which Alexandria was the largest harbour in the Levant; all the transit trade for merchandise from east Asia, Persia and India was concentrated there. The latter came by water across the Red Sea, then to the Nile and down. Cairo, the newly built capital, soon grew very prosperous and vied in fame with the two other Islamic capitals, Cordova and Baghdad. Even the collapse of the Fatimid regime in 1171 did not interrupt its brilliant development.

The dynasty lost its hold on its North African homeland by the conquest of Egypt; the governors who had been left behind in charge there seized their independence in the 11th century. Yet these provinces maintained some cultural relations with Cairo until the Almohads brought them completely into the Moorish sphere. Sicily also was lost to the Normans in 1071, but the artistic activity of the Saracens long continued to flourish there undisturbed and, despite many idiosyncrasies, belongs likewise in the Fatimid tradition.

Fortresses and Palaces

The new residence erected north of Fostat in the Nile country was first no more than a fortified precinct approachable only by troops and officials, about 1100 metres square; but it soon grew beyond this. The first town wall had been built of mud bricks; the second was put up by Syrian architects between 1087 and 1093 in a much more military style on the Byzantine model, with freestone facing, predominantly square towers and massive gate-houses, of which three are still standing. Each one is flanked in a different fashion by two strongly projecting towers, and opens in a large round-arched portal (plate 18a). The Bab Futuh shows over the entrance the earliest example of a flat dressed stone cupola over spherical pendentives. From here to the next gate, Bab Nasr, the whole extent of the wall has been exposed by Cresswell's excavations, and the system of fortification has thus been made clear in every detail (plate 18b).

The palaces of the Fatimids are known to us only from descriptions; these give us a fairy-tale impression of their splendour, but no conclusive facts about the type of layout. Mahdiya on the Tunisian coast was founded in 915 and served the dynasty as a capital until their removal to Egypt, but of the 'castle with the golden windows' barely a trace remains. No more can the exact disposition of the two residences which faced each other in Cairo be established. The larger, so-called Eastern Palace, with nine gates and a main façade 345 metres long was built by 973, and the smaller Western Palace was also completed before the end of the 10th century. It was built with two wings to surround a broad forecourt. The dominance of Persian influence can be guessed from the names given to some of the individual buildings both in Sabra and in Qairawan: al-Iwan and Khawarnaq (after a Sasanid castle of the 5th century).

The ruins excavated by General de Beylié in the Qal'a of Beni Hammad offer some compensation for the loss of the Fatimid remains in Cairo. Beni Hammad was a Fatimid governor who seized power in central Algeria. The main features of the one-time Dar al-Bahr (Sea Palace) can be recognized as a gigantic water tank occupying the whole of an arcaded courtyard, and the great throne room, besides a number of smaller rooms, baths, etc. The more loftily sited, citadel-like 'Lighthouse Castle' is interesting for the enlivening of the exterior with broad vertical fluting, and a cruciform dome chamber with niche recesses roofed with barrel vaults.

Lastly we may turn to the few remains of Arabo-Norman palaces in Palermo to complete our impression of the secular architecture of the Fatimid period. We know the older famous Fawara and the palace of Roger II (d. 1154) only from descriptions; but two pavilions finished under William II, the Zisa and the Cuba (1180) are preserved. The latter is a domed hall—its name derived from *qubba*—with two side rooms on a rectangular ground plan. There are salient blocks and vertical grooving similar to the Hammadite castle, but it is shallower here and runs up into pointed arches (plate 19a). The Zisa (from *Al-'Aziza*) is plainer outside, but rather more complicated in plan, with a central hall reaching through two storeys, and broadened by alcoves. Smaller living rooms were arranged round it and a second larger hall lay above it. The stalactite motif (*muqarnas*) is used here to great architectonic effect, filling the vaulting of the alcoves with corbelled, or over-hanging, rings of cells. It is an offshoot of the great development of the stalactite which was to take place both in Moorish and in Seljuk art.

Sacred Building

At the mosque in Mahdiya the most striking feature is the stately gatehouse, of a form hitherto scarcely known. The sanctuary roof rests on columns, while the arcades of the courtyard are formed of pointed arches on built-up piers. Of the mosque in the Hammadite city at least the minaret is partially preserved; it stood, as was customary in the Mahgreb, in the outer courtyard wall on the axis of the *mihrab*. On its southern side it is decorated with narrow arched recesses, tapering towards the top. In this decoration the same oriental influence is to be seen as on the façades of the secular buildings just described.

The Fatimid mosque in Cairo is related both to the Ibn Tulun, and to Sidi 'Oqba; the latter connection is particularly apparent in the broadening of the transept which runs up to the *mihrab*. Also stone is again used to a great extent, and a noteworthy architectural innovation is the emphasis on the façade, hitherto quite unknown.

Al-Azhar, the oldest Fatimid mosque in Cairo, was built as early as 970–972, but its original appearance has suffered much from its later transformation into an educational institution. The decorative four-centred arches of the court façades are old (plate 20a); they were perhaps introduced at that time into Egypt by a Persian architect. So are the aisles of the sanctuary which have pointed arches, with a broader *mihrab* nave flanked by double columns, probably under the influence of Qairawan. The two domes are raised over octagonal drums, formed from the quadrilateral by pointed niches in the corners. Al-Azhar is famous as the largest and oldest surviving Muslim university; lectures are delivered today in the great *haram*, just as they were almost a thousand years ago (plate 20b).

The mosque of al-Hakim was erected between 990 and 1003 on the model of the Ibn Tulun, and on a comparable scale. It has brick piers in the sanctuary, no transept, and a square dome chamber in front of the *mihrab* with transitional niches acting as squinches, as at al-Azhar. The enclosing wall is of stone, the façade unfortunately built up. The barrel-vaulted gateway has a pointed arch between salient flanking walls and is articulated by a series of shallow niches (plate 19b). At the two corners stand the towers, not in perfect preservation, one cylindrical on a square base with an internal spiral staircase, divided by windows and friezes of ornament into several storeys, the other first square, then octagonal with tapering storeys, and thus the prototype of all later Cairene minarets. Both have lost their tops; together with the strongly fortified gatehouse they give a pronounced military character to the Hakim façade.

The third important Fatimid mosque is Al-Aqmar. It was not

completed until 1125. The simple sanctuary with pointed arches on columns taken from despoiled buildings is less interesting than the richly animated façade which was to make history in Cairo. It is divided up into niches which at the top end with a bunch of rays in shell form—this motif later became one of the chief components of minaret decoration—and it also contains the first example of stalactite ornament on Egyptian soil. Besides these mosques there are several small Fatimid oratories (Giyushi, 1085, on the heights of the Mokattam which dominates the town; Salih Tala'i, 1160) which deserve attention on account of their decoration, and the few surviving mausolea, among which is that of Sayda Ruqaya of 1132. It is a tomb chapel of three rooms with a vestibule and a small courtyard; the cenotaph stood beneath the domed central room.

Stone, Stucco and Wood Carving

The stone which came into such extensive use for decorating the façades of Cairene mosques was of course often carefully ornamented, and apparently inspiration was sought in the first place from Moorish models; for many of the surviving monuments resemble the more or less contemporary Madinat az-Zahra in the treatment of the surface and the handling of vine scrolls. A striking example is the ornament on the façade of al-Hakim (plate 19b). The splendid open-work rosette at al-Aqmar shows how far Madinat was surpassed by Egypt in technical virtuosity. The same spirit is at work in the stucco decoration which predominates inside the buildings: on the friezes, mihrab panels, dome pendentives, windows etc. It seems at times to turn away from the Abbasid tradition designedly, so as to develop the Moorish-style arabesque scrolls more intensively. Often the two sources can be seen working together, until at last a new style of ornament arises, which has certainly used the Tulunid motifs, but has finally rejected the bevelled style. The use of epigraphy now becomes of prime importance; it appears everywhere, in a floriated interlaced decorative Kufic over a gentle arabesque background, giving rise to examples of astonishing calligraphic beauty. Characteristic of the successful fusion are the bands of stucco decorating the arches of the mosque of Salih Tala'i, just as in the Ibn Tulun: bands of script over feathery leaf work, which cannot belie its Cordovan origin. The *mihrab* wall is of course especially richly conceived, and gives scope for the most sumptuous decoration; it sometimes happens that the niche itself is no longer recessed, but is kept flat, with a mere suggestion of pillars, arches and frames or jambs in relief.

The development of wood decoration was more straight-forward. Since there was no question of Moorish influences here, it contrived to build on Tulunid foundations; gradually the bevelled or slant cutting became deeper, the vine scrollery became looser and prettier, and, before the danger-point of excessive luxuriance had been reached, it was bound into small polygonal panels combined into coffers. This conversion occurred less of course on roof beams and friezes than on doors, pulpits, cupboards and prayer niches; many of the latter were made of wood in Cairo at this time, and three of these 'transportable' *mihrabs* of the 12th century from al-Azhar, Sayda Ruqaya and Sayda Nefisa are preserved in the Islamic Museum in Cairo. With these belong several fine pulpits, one of which, finished in 1091 for the Husam mosque in Askalon, now stands in Hebron; another, from the year 1155 with very rich ornamental carving, is in the 'Amr mosque in Kus on the Upper Nile. The best preserved example of a *maqsura* for the prince is in the mosque of Qairawan; it was commissioned in 1040 and shows a survival of Abbasid traditions combined with a sense of style entirely parallel to the Fatimid. The door of the Martorana in Palermo proves how faithfully the Cairene style was transferred to Sicily (plate 22c). It was henceforth used for cenotaphs as well as for the parts of buildings and furniture already mentioned; these were preferred in wood and were effectively decorated with epigraphy.

The services required of carving in secular buildings were especially advantageous to its development along lines which would be unthinkable in the context of religious commissions. Large frieze boards were transferred from the West Palace in Cairo to the Qalaun building (see p. 116), erected later on the same site; because of this renewed use they were for long thought to be Mamluk work, but in fact there is no doubt that they belong to the zenith of the Fatimid period in the early 12th century. Here, arranged in cartouches and rosettes, are figured motifs of many kinds: musicians, dancing girls, revellers, falconers, hunting scenes etc, rendered with a truth to nature only thinkable under the tolerant aegis of the Shi'a, closely observed and skilfully picked out against the background (plate 21). Equally fine carvings of this kind were made for the Coptic church of Sayda Barbara, and can now be seen in the Coptic Museum in Old Cairo; in general the indigenous Christians seem to have accommodated themselves unreservedly to the prevalent Islamic style of the time in the fitting out of their churches.

The woodwork on mosque ceilings was now often decorated with painting; we have in fact no examples from Egypt, but there are some on the roofing of Sidi 'Oqba in Qairawan, which was restored at that time entirely in Fatimid style. More important is the ceiling of the Cappella Palatina in Palermo. The central aisle has several rows of stalactite vaulting which merges into coffering with sunk octagonal stars. The innumerable small surfaces created by this sculptural extravagance are thereupon all painted over in gay colours or gilded, some with inscriptions and arabesques, some with animal motifs over scrolls, but for the most part with a great variety of figured representations. Some of them treat themes similar to those on the carvings just mentioned in the Fatimid palace, but others introduce definite compositions of a more narrative nature. There can be no doubt that the whole ceiling is pure Saracen work, ordered by King Roger II for his palace chapel, which otherwise kept to Christian forms; the paintings are particularly valuable as a substitute for what has been lost in Egypt. For, according to reports of Arab authors, a very lively school of painting must have arisen at that time in Cairo, which even tackled figured motifs – always in an architectural context, it is true—and *inter alia* seems already to be using interesting illusionist techniques, not to speak of its achievement in book miniatures. It seems on the face of it possible that several master craftsmen were sent for from Cairo to Palermo.

Fatimid Applied Art

Oriental ivory work was, as earlier, especially coveted in the West, and among the many so-called oliphant horns and treasure boxes which have survived there is an Islamic group which bears the unmistakable stamp of Fatimid technique in its carving, with roundels of animals, hunting scenes, borders of vine scrolls etc (plate 22a). They were most likely made not in Egypt itself, but in the Saracen-influenced workshops of southern Italy which enjoyed lively encouragement throughout the Norman period. On the other hand the ivory plaques in openwork with very lively figures, similar to the wooden plaques from the Moristan of Qalaun (see above) are to be identified as Cairene work of the 12th century (plate 22b). In Sicily the painting and gilding of chests and pyxes of ivory was a speciality carried on well into the 13th century (plate 23b), with animals, revellers, falconers and such-like, besides Arabic benedictions for the owner. In yet other examples the motifs are accommodated to church use by the intro-duction of figures of saints.

The most outstanding achievement of the applied art of the period is the cutting of rock crystal for ewers, basins, smaller containers and chessmen. These were regarded as the wonder of oriental craftsmanship; they reached our church treasures through Levantine trade, pilgrimages and crusades. They were often made in Western style and used in celebration of the Mass, or as re-liquaries (plate 24a). Among them are pieces of considerable size, decorated in low relief, with animals, birds, plant scrolls and inscriptions; we may believe the Arab storytellers who relate how the Fatimid Caliphs possessed thousands of pieces of these costly vessels in their treasure chambers. The material is unknown in other Islamic countries, except for Iraq, and was no longer worked even in Egypt in later times.

This semi-precious stone was always difficult to obtain, and as a substitute objects were made of heavy lumps of glass and carved with the identical vigorous relief. Among these were goblets which became associated with the wine miracle of Saint Hedwig, Duchess of Silesia (so-called Hedwig goblets, plate 24b); she had presumably purchased them on her pilgrimage to the Holy Land. At the same time the technique of tonged and mould-blown decoration on bottles, bowls, dishes and so on was perfected, and lustre painting was adopted from pottery and applied to glass.

The advances made in Egypt in bronze technique were considerable. The shallow engraving used to decorate dishes, buckets, candlesticks, incense burners, footstools and other types of vessel, some of new form, remained within the usual repertoire of the Fatimid style with good luck inscriptions and animal medallions; but there were also objects cast in the round in animal shapes (ewers, incense vessels, etc) which call for attention. The most imposing piece of this nature, a metre high, is the celebrated griffin in the Camposanto at Pisa. Its provenance is difficult to assess; it is alleged to have been brought from Egypt during the crusades (plate 25). The body of the animal is almost completely covered with softly engraved patterns and inscriptions.

Lustre faience dominated ceramics. After the decline of the Baghdad industry in the 11th and 12th centuries, Egypt took the lead in the Muslim world which was only later taken over by Persia and Spain. The material excavated in Old Cairo includes, among the earlier types, frequent human representations which sometimes fill the whole of a dish, and imposing animal figures. In the same rubbish heaps there were also fragments with Fatimid decoration which certainly came from Syria, and which serve to prove that neighbours of Egypt were also practising lustre technique at that time. In Cairo itself there was also great enthusiasm for Chinese ceramics, and run-over glazes and celadon-style pieces were produced. Attempts were repeatedly made to produce a hard transparent ware to replace true porcelain. Besides these, unglazed earthenwares were in use: water jugs with ornamental strainers in astonishing variety, lamps, bread moulds, etc.

The Textile Industry

Egypt was of old the classic land of linen weaving, and the products of the industry were the mainstay of her export trade until the late Middle Ages. Especially the fine linens and the open cambric weaves of Egyptian looms had an unrivalled reputation.

They were now made even more costly, embellished at manufacture with interwoven stripes of silk. The technique is an extremely refined version of coarser Coptic wool tapestry; it occupied many thousands of workers in the industrial regions of the Nile delta (Tinnis and Damietta *inter alia*). Even before the Tulunids, state factories (*tiraz*) had been set up alongside private businesses. They had to meet all the requirements of the Baghdad court and of the bureaucracy for linen cloth, and now in the Fatimid period their exemplary organization attained remarkable productivity. There were some especially costly stuffs, interwoven with gold, which were to be produced exclusively for the Caliphs themselves, but even the luxury permitted to ordinary mortals seems to have been exceedingly lavish, as can be judged from the grave goods found in the cemeteries of Fostat and Upper Egypt. Shirts and over-garments, girdles and turban cloths were embellished with broad stripes of close silk embroidery in fine needlework, and by the 12th century this covered such large areas that the linen background was scarcely to be seen (plate 23a). The bestowal of robes of honour (the *khila'a*) was for long the customary sign of the ruler's favour in Islamic lands, and cloths were always the first choice for gifts to foreign potentates as well. The Intendant of the *Tiraz* ranked among the highest dignitaries, and on the occasion of a royal wedding or other such function his workshops had to produce thousands of pieces, often in a very short time.

In Sicily under the Normans, as in Egypt, a state manufacture (*regium ergasterium*) was carried on which seems to have had a monopoly in the production of gold borders (*aurifrisia*), woven ribbons with patterns in silk on a gold ground or vice versa. Byzantine features are stronger than Islamic in the motifs; this is because the pieces were destined chiefly as trimmings for costly vestments for the Western church; but on the other hand the embroidery seems to have been entirely in Saracen hands. The most splendid example of this technique that has survived from the Orient is the coronation mantle in the German Imperial Official Wardrobe, which according to an Arabic circular inscription was made for King Roger II in Palermo in the year 528 H (1133). On either side of a palm tree is a mirror repeat of a lion attacking a camel, composed within a semicircle with an extremely impressive and sophisticated stylization. The workshops concerned with commissions of this kind for the court are expressly designated as *palatio adhaerentes officinae*, and thus clearly had the same function as the Fatimid *tiraz*.

As far as woven silk is concerned, the share of Sicily in the surviving mediaeval material has been much overrated in the past. We have no convincing reason to doubt the correctness of the account that it was not until 1147, after the Norman campaigns against Greece, that the manufacture began with the help of craftsmen captured as 'booty'. It must indeed very soon have been transferred into the hands of Muslim craftsmen; for the designs of the 12th century that can be ascribed to it with certainty, though they certainly show reminiscences of Byzantium, are recast in a pronouncedly Islamic style and have correct Arabic script. Two-colour and multi-coloured weaves with repeats of double-headed eagles, confronted peacocks, panthers or other animals seem, as in the Seljuk realm (see below), to have been particularly favoured. From this work, which flourished well into the 13th century, grew the famous Gothic silver and gold brocades of Lucca and Venice, which can never belie their Sicilian-Saracenic origin.

CHAPTER FOUR

Seljuk Art

THE Seljuks were Turkmenian nomads from the Khirgis Steppe who entered Bukhara and Persia, and settled there. With their rise to power the Turkish element became dominant in the Islamic Orient. On the religious front they disputed the matter of Sunnite orthodoxy with the Shi'ite Persians and set themselves up as protectors of the Abbasids, who, bereft of all political power, looked sympathetically upon the new state. Thus in 1055 Tughril Beg was able to have himself proclaimed Sultan under the eyes of the Caliph in Baghdad, and soon to unite the whole of western Asia under his sway. At the end of the 11th century his empire broke into separate states, in which members of the Seljuk families and the generals (Atabegs) installed by them as governors founded new dynasties; in the 13th century these were all swept away by the Mongol invasion.

Artistic activity was lively in many of the princely courts set up at that time. Its greatest successes were in Persia, Mesopotamia and Asia Minor. The Turks themselves were rarely creative; they contented themselves with encouraging the indigenous arts by large-scale commissions. Even so their patronage was decisive in the change of style which indubitably occurs at this time: architecture becomes more monumental with increased emphasis on the effects of space arrangement; decoration becomes more sculptural, and the figures find their characteristic Islamic formulation.

The new attitude is most clearly noticeable in Asia Minor, which was not torn from the Byzantine empire until the beginning of

76

the 13th century and was untrammelled by any Islamic atavism. The capital, Konia, under Ala ed-din I, 'Sultan of Rum', became a cultural centre of great historic importance. Armenia too was at that time in Seljuk hands, and in the Mesopotamian highlands the Ortokids distinguished themselves as patrons, though even their zeal for art was surpassed by the Atabeg dynasties of the Zengids in Mosul and Syria. The strong personality of Nur ed-din (1146–1173) gave a new impetus to architecture and crafts in Aleppo and Damascus. The great Salah ed-din (Saladin) grew up at his court, and was intent on preserving the Seljuk tradition in Syria when he later founded the Ayyubid empire, so that the political union of this country with Egypt had little effect on its cultural life until afterwards, under the Mamluks.

Tombs

In Western Asia under the Seljuks the importance of the mausoleum grew to equal that of the mosque. It took two parallel forms, the funerary tower and the domed tomb, both of which developed in eastern Persia, in Khorasan, where they were erected as the sepulchres of Persian or Turkish princes or governors.

The funerary towers are thought to derive from the plain pre-Islamic structures of this kind which, favoured by conservative taste, survived the Abbasid regime, and were now elaborated into monumental buildings of brick. It is uncertain whether the round or faceted form is entitled to lay claim to the greater antiquity; certainly the earliest known monument belongs to the latter: the Bunbad-i-Qabus in Gurgan. It was erected in 985 on a star-shaped ground plan, slightly tapering in elevation and with a steep raking pointed roof. Its strict and simple form is very effective (plate 27a). Later, however, it was precisely in western Persia that the polygonal type was preferred (four, eight or ten sided); the finest of the surviving examples here is certainly the mausoleum of Mumine Khatun in Nakhichevan, built in 1186, with tall shallow recesses breaking up the surface. The round type with conical roof was particularly popular in Persia, both with a smooth body or with deep vertical fluting made by angled or round pillars, which give the exterior the aspect of a parade tent.

Inside it had a dome (for example in Radkan, in Rayy near Teheran, plate 27b). It is understandable that the Turkish potentates should wish their tombs to recall the tents which dominated their culture in life.

In Armenia the Seljuk round tower followed the architectural tradition that had formed in the Christian period; it was built in concrete with freestone facing, slightly profiled on the outside (*inter alia* the mausoleum in Akhlat). In Asia Minor these *turbe* are mostly faceted, and appointed rather simply, in contrast to the rich decoration of the Persian monuments which we shall deal with shortly. In Mesopotamia as well, the tombs of the saints were probably very modest until the Seljuk period when they took on a monumental character. In the region of Mosul we find them with a cubical base and a tall tent-shaped roof, sometimes with a vestibule, and in Iraq a highly individual roof prevailed: a tower-like pyramid rising in a number of zones of cells, with alternating arches carrying internally overhanging pointed niches. In the Imam Dar near Takrit we find it on a quadrilateral plinth, while in the most famous example, the tomb of Sitta Zubaida near Baghdad, it rises over an eight-sided prism which is also octagonal inside (plate 28a). It is quite possible that this mausoleum rightly bears the name of the wife of the Caliph Harun ar-Rashid, though in its present form it is unlikely to have been erected until some time during the 12th century, when the *muqarnas* motif had already grown into a logical architectural form. The tomb of Nur ed-din in the *madrasah* named after him in Damascus is very similar, vaulted over with concentric rings of cells. It demonstrates how widely this feature was being disseminated.

The inspiration for the great domed mausolea is rightly traced by Diez back to the time-honoured domed dwelling house customary in the Persian desert towns. In Khorasan this house had developed a corner squinch vaulting, growing out from the corners of the walls in arched courses of brick. These now were used alongside the niched or celled domes already mentioned. During its development the squinch took over the task of producing an octagonal drum and gallery zone, above which the bowl of the dome was laid. The mausoleum of the Sultan Sanjar, who died in 1157, stands imposingly among the ruins of the Seljuk town at Merv. Here the squinches have created a gallery zone,with a double row of niches round the dome. Seen from outside, the structure appears simply as a smooth shell above the drum, and gives no indication of the noble scale of the interior vaulting. The ruined building preserved in Tus, the ancient residence of Khorasan, with its *iwan*-like entrance, oblong fluted recesses in the sides and octagonal gallery supporting the dome is said to be the tomb of the famous theologian Ghazali, who died in 1111 (plate 28b).

Madrasah and Mosque

The Seljuks introduced a second type of sacred building into Islamic architecture in the shape of colleges (*madrasah*) which, in contrast with the University (*Dar el-'ilm*) were to serve entirely the public dissemination of the traditional teaching and the formation of a class of officials well versed in it. Inside Persia, the stronghold of the Shi'ite sect, the Imam Shafi'i, one of the great orthodox teachers of the law, created cult centres of the Sunnite sect, but it was not until the Turkish supremacy that the academies founded by him received official sanction or a worthy architectural frame. The greatest supporter and builder of such institutes was the Seljuk vizir Nizam el-Mulk; he also deserves credit as patron of the great thinker Omar Khayyam. He established *madrasah* in Nishapur, Tus and Baghdad (the latter in 1066) and his example was followed by other important personages who piously endowed establishments with secure incomes, so that the number of towns possessing them could be counted in dozens. Unfortunately not one of them is preserved in Persia from this period. They were there exclusively dedicated to the Shafi'ite teaching, whereas the Zengids in Mosul and Syria favoured the Hanafite rite and in Iraq the Hanbalite doctrine was dominant; the fourth orthodoxy, that of the Malekites, was confined to the Mahgreb. The plan to unite all four doctrines in a common Academy was carried out by the last-but-one Abbasid, al-Mustansir, in 1232 in the great *madrasah* of Baghdad named after him. Only ruins remain. Round an elongated rectangular courtyard rose an *iwan* about 6 metres broad in the middle of each side, flanked on either long side by further halls which evidently served as lecture halls, separated from the *iwan* by a closed chamber. Between each block were the cubicles for the students in two storeys, behind arcades of four-centred arches on pillars (fig 11).

In Asia Minor the college buildings of the Seljuks survive in great numbers. They are not so stately in their layout as in Persia, but they are interesting for their concern with the problem of the dome. Two kinds are distinguished there, in which the connection between the school and the founder's tomb was the regulating

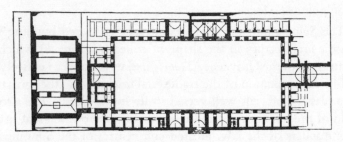

11. Plan of the Mustansiriya *madrasah* in Baghdad after Herzfeld (*Archäologische Reise* II, p. 166). More recent work seems to show that this ground plan needs revising in a few particulars.

factor: one with an *iwan* (vaulted three-sided hall) and forecourt, the other with a dome chamber and water basin instead of the open fountain court. There are especially instructive examples in the ancient residence of Konia. The Sircali *madrasah* (1242) has an *iwan* with prayer niche, flanked by two dome chambers with a simple, patently Turkish style of vaulting in the tomb chamber: the transition from the square to the octagon is effected by a zone of alternately projecting and receding triangles. This method of construction remained customary all over Anatolia except where it was replaced by the Byzantine pendentive dome. In the Karatay *madrasah* (1251) the only surviving part of the original building is the dome chamber with the lecture hall and the tomb area to the left of it. The transition to the round is worked here through fan brackets of brick, a method which occurs in other examples and is considered to be a solution introduced from India through Central Asia.

Nur ed-din concerned himself with founding *madrasah* in Syria; besides the Nuriye (1172) already mentioned, most of the school buildings in Damascus, Aleppo, Hama, Baalbek and other places, all unfortunately badly or not at all preserved, can be traced back to him. Saladin for his part carried the form from here to Egypt (see below).

It was inevitable that the centrally focused and symmetrically planned building thus achieved should be combined with the idea of the dome. Transferred to the mosque it opened up new possibilities of development towards monumentality. This evolution took place in Persia, and that is why the *madrasah* is so important in the history of architecture. First a new ordering of space was achieved by using the ground plan of the *madrasah* over the traditional early Islamic courtyard plan. The obligatory four barrel-vaulted *iwan*, together with the niched walls joining them, now make the mosque courtyard look like that of a law school; the only difference is in what lies behind the façade of niches: not the cells of the students but pillared halls for the faithful; the upper storey is usually built as a gallery. The 'new type' prevailed more and more under the Seljuks; the great Sultan's mosque of Malik Shah, built in Baghdad in 1092 must already have been built according to this plan, with large *iwan*; this supposition is supported by the Friday Mosque in Isfahan, rebuilt by the same ruler from earlier remains (fig 12). Later it underwent further extensive alterations, but of the Seljuk period at least the southern dome remains, with the gigantically wide *iwan* in front of it.

Otherwise in Mesopotamia the pillared hall with flat roof was generally retained, and ideas from Persia were only adopted piecemeal and rather timidly. In Mosul the Great Mosque of Nur ed-din was built in two periods, 1148 and 1170–1172. It was on octagonal piers and, clearly, was vaulted; the only part surviving is the southern aisle along the *qibla* wall with the *mihrab* of 1148 (a second, later prayer niche stands in the courtyard, which must therefore have been used as a *musalla*, or open sanctuary). The minaret is of brick, cylindrical over a cubical plinth, with a helmet-

6

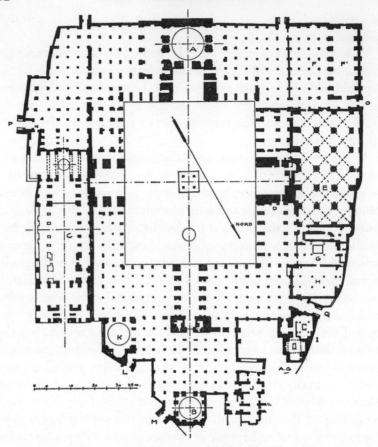

12. The plan by A. Godard (*Historique de Masdjid-e Djum'ad'Isfahan*, in *Athâr-e Irân* I, 2, 1936, pp. 213 ff) makes clear the different periods of building: between 1072 and 1092 the Seljuk kiosk mosque; in the 12th century conversion to a 4-*iwan* mosque; 1310 the stucco *mihrab* of Uljaitu; 1366 the addition of several out-buildings under the Muzaffarids; 1475 ceramic decoration of the southern iwan and the court façade.

like roof. We can see how varied were the mosque towers at this time in Mesopotamia; in Balis is an eight-sided, tall minaret with window slits at the turns of the steps; in Baghdad, preserved in the Suq el-Ghazl, is one much more squat, which originally belonged to the small Caliph's Mosque, but was added to in the early 13th century entirely in Seljuk style. In its upper half the cylindrical body was set about with row upon row of overhanging stalactites.

In Damascus, and in fact all over Syria, the flat-roofed mosque without transept was retained; the *qubba* was reserved solely for the tomb chamber and not before the mosque of Rukn ed-din (1224) do we find a dome-roofed court. It was much the same in Asia Minor, where wood supports were still used at first for the *haram*, and columns or pillars of stone were not generally used until later. The buttresses on the outer wall were brought into a rhythmical arrangement with the help of windows and recesses to make a simple ordering of the façade, to which an artistic focus was then given by adding gates of honour. Open courtyards with arcades were rare here; they were content as a rule with very modest forecourts. The chief mosque in Siwas is also very unpretentious, and the castle mosque in Konia, a pillared building with a dome, of the year 1209, is hardly remarkable as architecture. In Armenia there are two buildings which deserve mention: the Ulu Jami' in Van, a pillared hall of the 12th-13th century with a *mihrab* dome, and the mosque at Ani (c. 1100) which is noteworthy for the sanctuary which consists of several sections each independently vaulted and supported by squat round pillars.

Secular Building

The Seljuks as a military power naturally set great store by strong fortresses, which indeed were rendered essential by the presence of Byzantium on the western frontier and the activities of the crusaders. The chief task of the Zengid Nur ed-din was the completion of the town wall and citadel of Damascus. The grandiose and picturesque castle of Aleppo (plate 29) (which, though much restored in the 13th century is still essentially his) is the most telling example of the daring feats of architectural imagination to which the potentate was able to incite the art of engineering. Under Saladin, fortresses were still the first priority in Syria, and their carefully thought-out fortifications spelt failure for all the attacks of the Franks. Jerusalem too, after its conquest in 1187, was strongly fortified; the impressive Damascus gate is worthy to take its place among the Zengid buildings.

The town wall of Konia with its 108 towers, built by Ala ed-din in 1221, is now completely destroyed; it was no less con-siderable than that of Amida which was continually being strengthened during the 11th and 12th centuries with towers and bastions, in stages which can be clearly traced from the building inscriptions. The renovations on the Abbasid walls of Baghdad were mostly Seljuk work. They were still standing, with a few later restorations, in the middle of the 19th century, when they were pulled down except for two gates. These belong to the important building work executed between 1180 and 1225, and still show the ancient structure with its imposing bastions.

As for palace building, the residences of the great Seljuks in Nishapur and Merv have disappeared irrevocably, and so have those of the many smaller dynasties in Persia. The *iwan* of the Qal'a still standing in Baghdad is part of a palace more or less contemporary with the two gates, and is worthy of mention be-cause of its decoration. The Qara Saray is preserved in Mosul from the Zengid castle; there are ruins of a barrel vaulted hall, which must originally have formed an open *iwan*, built about 1233 under the splendour-loving Atabeg L'ul'u. In Syria there are no princely buildings of this time, and in Konia there remain the ruins of a tower with a loggia-like superstructure on mighty stalactite brackets which belonged to the residence erected between 1156 and 1188. Further remains of palaces in Anatolia await more exact survey.

The main survivals from Seljuk secular building are the caravan-serais (*han*) which were placed systematically on all important routes in place of the more primitive inns usual until then. They were often very stately establishments. They certainly were an important influence in the formation of the *madrasah*, which have not unjustly been called 'academic *han*'; unfortunately there are no early examples left to prove this. The most usual type arose in Persia, but is now only to be met with in any numbers in Asia Minor, where it is a characteristic monument. They have recently been studied systematically and published by K. Erdmann.

Vaulted galleries and rooms were laid out round a rectangular courtyard entered through a central portal, and the centre was

usually occupied by a small oratorium. In the most famous
example, the Sultan Han on the road to Konia (1229), an elongated
pillared hall, five aisles broad, with arched vaulting and a small
central dome is attached to the courtyard, and may have served as
a warehouse (fig 13). The gate is flanked by recesses and the walls

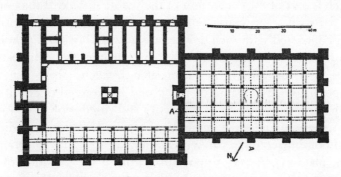

13. The Sultan Han near Aksaray on the road to Konia, after Sarre (*Denkmäler
persischer Baukunst*). Recently exhaustively published by K. Erdmann (*Das
anatolische Karawansaray des 13. Jahrhunderts*, Berlin, 1961, Nr 25). The building
has an enclosing wall with massive towers, a hall with several aisles and a forecourt
with a small mosque in the centre. According to an inscription it was built in 1229
and restored in 1278.

are armed with corner towers and buttresses. In Mesopotamia,
between Sinjar and Mosul, there still stands a mid-13th century
building known as Al-khan. It is rectangular, with round corner
towers and vaulted rooms.

Decoration in Stone, Stucco and Wood

In all the Seljuk buildings in Asia Minor—mosques, *madrasah*,
palaces and caravanserais—the layout of the gateway is of special
importance; the highly varied decorative arrangements give an
individual stamp to each building. Structural problems recede
into the background; in place of the imposing Persian *iwan* we
have here stone portals of less ambitious dimensions, but which
retain a monumental note in the manner of their treatment. In the
first examples the builder was content with a simple pointed
arched opening, but soon new designs were adopted. The recesses
are vaulted with overhanging rows of stalactites, making them

rather like a fireplace in appearance, and set in rectangular frames, faced with plaques of profuse, rather flat polygonal ornament. Sircali *madrasah*, Laranda mosque (plate 30a), Sultan Han and many other buildings have portals of this type.

In other cases the recess almost vanishes in a more gentle curve which is part of the decoration of the whole surface of the portal; the flat stripes and bands with script and geometric designs are then contrasted with such devices as knots, ribbons and palmettes in a higher, more sculptural relief (e.g. in Inje Minareli). Sometimes, and surprisingly not in a later decadent phase but contemporaneous, the frame of the portal is plastered over with an inorganic superstructure of palmettes and rosettes of most varied form, perhaps under the influence of certain church façades in the neighbouring country of Armenia (cf. the mosque in Diwrigi, 1228, plate 31). A very important feature is the inclusion of the minaret in the portal structure, with its logical outcome in the twin minarets growing out of the portal (Shifte minaret and Gök Madrasah in Siwas, 1271, *inter alia*; they are often ruined, cf. Laranda mosque in Konia, plate 30a). They already show the broadly stepped, or narrower fluted needle shape, interrupted by a gallery on a capital-like stalactite bracket. This device was later adopted by the Ottoman architects for the mosques of Constantinople. In Mesopotamia and Syria the portals were of less importance to the appearance of the building; but here the *mihrab* walls were often furnished with rich stone decoration.

The same Turks, who were so concerned to counter the Shi'ite confession in Persia by founding orthodox *madrasah*, showed a lack of scruple on the question of figured motifs which in no way corresponded to the stricter Sunnite observance. This was probably the result of influences reaching them from eastern Turkestan. Just at the time of their rule there occurs an unusual preference for animate themes, going even as far as modelling in the round, and the surviving examples are positive testimony to the interest taken in these things by various Seljuk rulers. This taste came to the fore chiefly in stucco decoration, and led on in Rayy and other Persian sites to the execution of high reliefs, some on a large scale. There are figures of watchmen or representations of enthroned princes with servants at their side; themes which concern primarily the decoration of palaces. The Talisman gate in Baghdad, dated to 1221, is a particularly interesting example of this tendency, transferred to stone; in the sitting figure between two lambent dragons some have seen the allegory of the Caliph subduing his enemies, while others regard it as having only apotropaic significance. In any case in this form it is certainly inspired by Chinese models which treated of the same theme in similar places, and in its turn it evoked at least related motifs in the sculpture surrounding Romanesque portals.

In the Qara Saray, which is all that remains of the residence of Atabeg L'ul'u in Mosul, the hall is decorated in stucco not with inscriptions and abstract ornament only but with rows of half-figures in niches; they may be traced back to Buddhist inspiration, of which there are other signs in Mesopotamia. In Asia Minor there are more frequent examples, and here stone sculpture is more common, alongside plaster friezes with lively battle scenes or smaller single animals. Here belong the powerfully modelled lions and other details from the Sultans' palace in Konia as well as reliefs in a more heraldic vein from the town wall. According to ancient reports this wall must have had an astonishingly rich figured decoration, using some motifs derived from the Antique and from Byzantium, and compiled with childish gaiety and quite without plan.

Seljuk applied art is reckoned at its most brilliant in the wooden furniture preserved in or acquired from the mosques of Asia Minor. The decoration is carved, sometimes in open work, with designs suitable for religious places of worship, and so of course confined to geometric and plant ornament and inscriptions, but executed with great artistry. Doors, pulpits (minbar), screens for private pews (maqsura), cenotaphs and lecterns (rahle) are the chief pieces. There is a large number of these, some very fine, from the best period of the 13th century in the museums of Istanbul and Ankara (plate 32). As a rule doors and pulpits have their panels decorated with polygonal patterning, while smaller objects tend to be treated more freely with arabesques and inscriptions. In this group belong the outstandingly stately minbar completed in

Aleppo in 1187, which Saladin commissioned for his improvements to the 'Aqsa mosque, and another in the mosque of Ala ed-din in Konia, dated 1155 (plate 33b). The panelling is carried out with particular care. There is an example of a relatively late wooden *mihrab* (dated 1245) with rich panelling, already anticipating the future Mamluk style, in the Halawiye *madrasah* in Aleppo.

Architectural Ceramics

The innovations introduced into Persian religious building during the Seljuk period found their principal ornamental expression in the decoration of the surface with ceramic. The oldest funerary and mosque towers had a simple brick patterning which could be adapted to epigraphic and ornamental effect, and brickwork was used in Iraq towards the end of the 12th century for interior decoration, achieving extraordinarily felicitous results in the Qal'a *iwan* in Baghdad. The surface is given the character of wood panelling by dividing it into angular sections, and the pattern itself, which is dominated by a central shield and four corner wedges, achieves the effect of a ceramic facing. Intricate arabesques are deeply carved into the terra cotta surface with a highly sculptural effect, and the lines are drawn with extraordinarily sure elegance. In the interior, use was also made of the much simpler technique of brick and stucco mosaic. The field was divided into a continuous polygonal diaper with glazed bricks, surrounding a filling of stucco palmettes. This is found in the ruins of the palace at Konia, and, particularly successfully, in the mausoleum of Mumine Khatun.

An extension of the ceramic methods so far known towards greater colour took place in the 13th century in Asia Minor with the use of faience mosaic, first (1220) on the *mihrab* and pendentives of the mosque of Aladin which is otherwise so plain, then in the courtyard of the Sircali *madrasah*, and at its most perfect in the tomb chamber of the Qaratay *madrasah* (1251), where unfortunately the lower wall-facing is missing. Here the whole dome is filled with a concentric star pattern, scattered, above and below, with quotations from the Koran in decorative Kufic script. At first only four colours are used: light blue, dark blue, brown and black; an extension of the palette took place in the following period in Persia. This is certainly where the new technique originated, and it is quite fortuitous that the oldest monuments to have survived are in Anatolia; indeed the name of the builder of several of them is expressly recorded as Muhammad of Tus, who is thus a native of Khorasan.

In Konia at this time the prayer niches were also furnished with faience mosaic. They resemble the portals in the shaping of their arches with overhanging stalactites in a sort of corbelling (plate 33a). In Persia on the other hand the suggestion of a niche in the flat *mihrab* is achieved by relief either in stucco or, the great innovation, in lustre tiles, which have both the metal colour and cobalt blue painting on white glaze. One of these lustre *mihrabs* is preserved in the Islamic section of the Berlin Museum; it carries the date 1226 and its provenance is authenticated from the Meidan mosque in Kashan; this is precisely the home of tile (*kashi, kahsani*) production in Persia (plate 34).

Calligraphy and Miniature Painting

Seljuk monuments show an enrichment in epigraphy over the previous period which is evident even to the layman: beside the angular, always ceremonious, branching and entwined Kufic there was also adopted a new round hand, called Naskhi, its swings and swellings in singular contrast to the lapidary style of lettering (cf. particularly plate 42a). It was originally only current as a cursive hand, but it received its calligraphic sanction at the hands of the great masters of the Baghdad school, and now became generally established, both in book production and on monuments, and also in inscriptions on vessels. In Konia it is found both in the stone carving of the portals and also in the difficult technique of faience mosaic, and it was practised from the 12th century in other countries too with great skill. On Persian tomb stones, however, an ornamental version of Kufic held its own for some time.

In book making the parchment used heretofore was now superseded by paper. It was produced first in Samarqand after Chinese models and soon production spread further. The Koran texts in steep or round hand, now always written in vertical format, were often embedded in a ground of arabesques for luxury copies, and the title pages gradually assumed especial decorative importance.

Baghdad's leading role was not confined to the innovations in calligraphy: it can boast the first Islamic school of miniature painting. It arose in association with the Arabic translations of Greek scientific works, in which explanatory pictures were interspersed through the text, and the style of painting thus evolved was now used to illustrate the popular entertainment literature of the time. This set new problems of composition and stimulated developments in the art of colouring. Thus from the 12th century we find alongside the writings of Dioscorides and Galen, the animal fables of Kalika and Dimna and the Anecdotes of Hariri in illustrated manuscripts which equal or even surpass contemporary Western book illuminations in allusive treatment of themes, in surety of drawing and effective use of colour. The roots of this sudden flowering of miniature painting have not yet been fully traced; they are certainly not to be sought solely in the Hellenistic and Byzantine past, but in the highly developed book art of the Manichaean monasteries of eastern Turkestan, with which the Uighur secretaries of the Seljuk generals were certainly familiar. They were at least partly instrumental in stimulating the new development.

In an edition of Dioscorides of 1224 the Arab painter has represented famous Greek doctors explaining a prescription to an amanuensis, or instructing in the preparation of a mixture (plate 35a); the often humorous conception, and the sure touch with its nuances of colour show the miniaturist entirely his own master. Two manuscripts of Hariri are particularly masterly: the witty conceits and rogueries of Abu Zayd of Sarruj are pictured with penetrating observation and a brilliant sense of composition. One, dated 1237, is in the Bibliothèque Nationale, the other is in Leningrad, both most revealing for details of mediaeval life in Islam. We see how mosques, libraries, dispensaries, courts of justice and shops were laid out, how festive processions and weddings were arranged and what the sailing boats looked like that people travelled in (plate 35b).

Seljuk Metalwork and Faience

The first examples of copper inlay in bronze are found, as we have seen, in the 'decadant' phase of Sasanid art which flourished chiefly in west Turkestan under the Samanids. Once again the new generation sees the ever-creative Khorasan in the lead. There the technique of copper and silver inlay was developed during the 11th and 12th centuries to produce such remarkable pieces as the bronze vessel preserved in Leningrad (plate 36), authenticated as Herat work of the year 1163. It has horizontal friezes in which are angular and round inscriptions, some of them 'animated', with the letters ending in human heads, and processions of riders, dancing girls, musicians and acrobats. At about the same time ewers and lamps were being worked in northern Mesopotamia or in Kurdistan in chased bronze with rows of lions or doves in relief. They have only very slight traces of inlay in the engraved surfaces, and at the beginning of the 13th century Mosul took the lead in metalwork under the active encouragement of the Zengids, and achieved extraordinary refinements of inlay technique.

Gold was now used as an inlay material as well as silver; the surface of the vessel is prepared by most delicate engraving and then adorned so carefully with strips of silver and gold that not a ripple of irregularity is left on the surface. As in lustre painting the prohibition of utensils of noble metals led to very interesting substitutes. We have the dates and names of several Mosul craftsmen on these fine vessels; it is therefore not surprising that the town has given its name to the whole class of fine oriental work called Mosul bronzes. In fact there are several signatures to prove conclusively that the technique was carried abroad from Mosul by craftsmen who settled in Baghdad, Aleppo, Damascus and Cairo, and also in Persia, thus founding new schools of inlay which never entirely belie their origins. Of the ewers, basins, dishes, vases and candlesticks which were thus made in the 13th century many were for Christian patrons; this is apparent in the use of figures of saints and biblical scenes (plate 37); from the signatures it can be deduced that a few of the craftsmen themselves were Christians.

The established skill of the Persian and Mesopotamian potters found great opportunities for fruitful activity in the Seljuk period. Not only were there the needs of architecture in ceramics to be met, but there was a steady demand for decorative ware. For this there were three chief centres which produced works of high quality in very varied techniques.

Mosul is the production centre, particularly in the 12th century, of lightly baked, unglazed earthenwares, which were decorated partly by incrustation, partly by incision and stamping, showing stylistic analogies with the local stucco work. In addition to bottles and jugs ornamented with applied medallions stabbed with graceful motifs, or with stamped animal friezes, they made very large water jars with high-relief inscriptions, human heads, seated Buddha-like figures and similar ornament.

There is no reliable evidence of ceramic activity at Raqqa on the Euphrates at the time of Harun ar Rashid, but in the 12th century Raqqa comes to the fore with several faience techniques which both in the paste and in the use of lead glazes are closer to the products of Syria than to those of Iraq. A brownish lustre was much used, and various colours; transparent turquoise green glazes with black drawing are particularly plentiful, and the good-wish inscriptions and palmettes are accompanied by charming stylized animal motifs and human figures. A speciality of Raqqa is a class of four- or six-sided drum-shaped vessels, decorated in relief and glazed turquoise green, which may have served for storing or warming food.

The most important potting town in the Seljuk period, and a cultural centre of the first rank, was the widely renowned Rayy near Teheran. Here the most advanced methods were carried on until the mid-13th century, producing luxury wares such as have rarely been equalled since. Rayy took over the lead in lustre production from Cairo, combining the most advanced techniques with superlative aesthetic sense to produce exquisite examples of this ware. Not content with this the Rayy potters injected new life into the rather undisciplined techniques of incision and relief (Gabri) which were declining into a folk art relying on watered-down Sasanid reminiscences; and in their Minai majolica they discovered, about the middle of the 12th century, an overglaze painting which in its polychrome effect rivals the contemporary Baghdad school of miniature painting (plate 38a). They also made splendid faiences with openwork encrusted decoration with leaf gilding, and lastly we have examples of the amazing perfection reached by the Rayy potters in their attempts to oust Sung porcelain, especially the white 'ting yao', with a transparent 'frit' on a hard paste. Figure motifs are current on Rayy ceramics; in general they are confined to the decorative use of throne scenes, riders, sphinxes etc; the Minai wares evolved the stereotyped presentation of genre motifs and subjects taken from Persian epic such as Bahram Gur hunting or Khosrau discovering Shirin.

Kashan is another important ceramic centre, where, in addition to the tiles already mentioned, vessels were produced inferior only to those of Rayy, and methods of making lustre ware were further perfected. Activity continued there into the Mongol period.

There is no doubt that enamelling and gilding on glass, a practice common in northern Syria since the 12th century, especially in Aleppo and probably also in Mesopotamia, owed its origin to the Seljuks. Drinking goblets seem to have had some symbolic meaning for Turkish nobles; they appear in every kind of surviving representation as a constant attribute in the hand of a reigning potentate, and have also been found in considerable numbers in Tartar graves in the Crimea, most probably imported from Syria (plate 38b). Large table ware, bottles, goblets, jugs and basins of various forms were also given the same decoration, for although the centres in question had by this time come under the sway of the Ayyubids, these rulers followed the policy they pursued in other spheres and left the Seljuk tradition to develop in its own way. The motifs belong entirely to the repertoire used on the faiences of Rayy and the bronzes of Mosul: friezes of revellers and musicians, horsemen with falcons, fighting or playing polo, animals pursuing or attacking each other, etc. They were carried out by artists possessed of great graphic skill and a fine sensitivity for the tonal values of the enamel colours. More modestly decorated goblets have only a band of inscription with benedictions or a band of abstract ornament, while others again have the whole surface covered with either close or loose arabesques in enamel with gilding. The renowned goblet of the ballad, the 'Luck of Edenhall', was just such a Syrian ceremonial goblet brought back from the Levant; it attained legendary fame and still exists, in excellent preservation, in the British Museum. Mosque hanging lamps which should be mentioned in relation to this period are rarely, and only then sparsely, decorated; they first became fashionable under the Mamluks (see p. 122).

Carpets and Textiles

The advance of the Seljuks made the civilization of western Asia acquainted with the knotted carpet. Until then it had simply been produced in the steppes by Turkmen nomadic tribes to protect themselves from the weather. It must have become naturalized as families of Seljuks forsook their nomadic ways and, settling down in certain places, continued and developed production on a business scale until it became integrated in the textile industry. It is to be supposed that this also happened early on in Persia, but the only evidence for the existence of knotting technique in the Seljuk period, apart from references in early writers, comes from Asia Minor; it consists of a few pieces which lay in the Ala ed-din mosque in Konia and are now the pride of the Istanbul Museum of Turkish and Islamic Art. They already show the feature characteristic of all later developments: the strong contrast between the field and border; the former either contains a continuous geometric pattern or smaller polygons repeated over the whole surface in regular rows; the border as a rule is a frieze of repeats of meaningless but extremely effective Kufic script (plate 37b). The knotting is still very rough, but the colour combination is highly sophisticated. The whole tremendous development of Anatolian knotted carpets arose from these beginnings.

The Baghdad silk industry owed its prosperity in the 10th and 11th centuries to the initiative of the Buyids, and subsequently under the Seljuks cloths of various kinds seem to have been manufactured there and elsewhere especially for export to the Christian West. Our terms 'baldachin' (Baghdad material) and 'muslin' are reminiscent of the lively trade relations existing at that period.

These products supplemented those from the Egyptian *tiraz* factories; two-colour silks were among the specialities of Iraq, though they met competition for the Western market from the looms of Palermo. Delicate silks and heavier brocades often show highly stylized confronted animals, griffins or lions, separated by an ornamental tree, enclosed by a circle of inscriptions or an animal frieze; this motif is usually in two variants arranged in rows in a continuous repeat; others repeat the motif of a double eagle in Ortukid style, and can therefore be attributed to northern Mesopotamia. There was also a very vigorous industry in Persia itself.

The Development of Islamic India

Both the prelude and post-lude of the Seljuk epoch are to be sought in Muslim India. In the empire set up by Mahmud of Ghazna (997–1028) at the turn of the millennium in what was previously Bactria, and which he extended towards Persia and Hindustan, art was already leaning towards a style which signified the transition from the post-Sasanian tradition to the trend adopted by the Seljuks. The Ghaznavids were Turks, but it was rather the Persian civilization that they cultivated; let us remember that it was under the auspices of Mahmud that Firdusi completed the great national epic; nor did they shut themselves off from the powerful impact of Buddhist monuments. They were driven from power by the Ghorids in the mid-12th century. It is only recently that a little evidence has been forthcoming of Ghorid artistic activity.

In Hindustan itself the so-called Pathan style grew up after 1200 under the dynasties of Turkish slave kings which followed. It was a movement which corresponded basically to Seljuk trends in art, though its individuality lay in the necessity of taking into account the peculiarities of Indian landscape. It took so deep a root that it continued into the 15th century unaffected by the deep changes wrought nearby in Persia by the Mongols. Delhi grew enormously in the 13th and 14th centuries; the princes embellished the town with more and more new buildings, and court life was characterized by the variety of nationalities among its officials, military officers and scholars who came from every Islamic country to achieve office and honour there.

The mausolea of the so-called Pathan period are unmistakably derived from the Persian domed tombs; they are generally heavy in form, four sided, tapering, and with four gates. Strongly battered enclosing walls with corner bastions gave them the character of fortified tomb-castles, and they retained this character until the end of the 14th century. The mausoleum raised by Muhammad

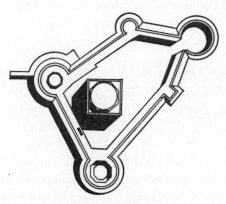

14. Fortified tomb of Tughlaq Shah (d. 1324) built by his son Muhammad. The mausoleum itself is a domed building with strongly battered walls of red sandstone with stripes of marble (After F. Wetzel, *Islamische Grabbauten in Indien*, Leipzig, 1918, pp. 31 f.)

Tughlaq near Delhi in 1325 for his father has part of the enclosure wall designed inside as a pillared corridor with eaves. The problem of the dome was not solved in the Persian fashion, but on the native principles which derived largely from wooden architecture, using *inter alia* wall brackets and groin vaulting.

It is not yet clear to what extent Muslim India contributed to the development of the *madrasah* and mosque. But the first state *madrasah* was built in Ghazna in the early 11th century, so that here Mahmud anticipated the Seljuk potentates. Otherwise special conditions obtained in India, and it is only with strict qualifications that its art can be associated with that of the Seljuks; the oratories of the great mosques of Delhi and Ajmir were built in the 13th century as adaptations of, or using spoil from, Jain temples; the form of the supports was influenced by these alien, sometimes bombastic fashions, for since the Jains did not represent living figures their work was acceptable to the Muslims. High walls with Persian pointed-arch gates were built to screen the pillared halls, and a *qibla* wall was planted right across the inner space, but otherwise many a typical Indian feature crept in, particularly as the workers employed on the building were predominantly Hindus, and only introduced foreign forms and practices when specifically ordered to do so. In the technique of building arches, for instance, the native tradition of corbelling was retained, for capitals the lotus form was preferred, and in constructing cupolas they used, as has been said, the methods acquired during past ages of wood building. Truly independent and harmoniously thought out plans for the mosque only came later.

The unusual Qutb minaret in Delhi (plate 30b) is an interesting attempt to create the national form of minaret by extending the Iranian-Seljuk fluted funerary tower into a mosque tower. It is strongly tapered and the deep fluting is vigorously tied in at intervals with broad collars. Rings of fine calligraphy in both angular and round hand lend it a particularly decorative note. On the gateway alongside (1310), the doors, lattice windows and blind niches form the architectural articulation of a surface which is completely covered with miniature script and other small abstract motifs in separate fields. In many respects the designs are related to the Moorish style (see below). The stone decoration even surpasses Seljuk work in Anatolia in exuberance.

There are many more secular buildings in India than in Persia, and there are grounds for hoping that more so-far unpublished examples will be added to those already known. More than elsewhere the buildings were subject to the conditions imposed by ground and climate, conditions which differed considerably from one site and landscape to another. The significance of the tall 'victory towers' of Ghazna, mistakenly held to be minarets, and their relationship to other buildings must remain undecided. In 1949 Schlumberger discovered a Ghaznevid palace in Lashkari Bazaar (Afghanistan) and provided the first information about dwellings of this period. In India itself the oldest examples are

7

planned round a courtyard with low pillared arcades and a main building of two storeys; they are completely without decoration and very massive, still very Hindu. In Delhi the famous 'thousand pillar castle' (Hezar Sutun) of 'Ala ed-din Khalji (c. 1300) cannot be identified, but there are remains of many other palaces among the ruins there. According to ancient descriptions the way in led through an outer gate-house with the Music Watch (Nubat Khane) to a second portal, which led to the courtyard and hall for those awaiting audience; lastly through a third to the Diwan i-'Am, the court of honour itself with the throne room. Firuz Shah (1351–1388) founded a new section of the town called Firuzabad, with many palaces, near Old Delhi.

Islamic India did not produce much of interest in applied arts at this time. It is noteworthy that the use of the round Naskhi hand in epigraphy began earlier here than in western Asia. The period of Mahmud of Ghazna is important for its influence on Seljuk style. One of the most interesting relics from this preceding, formative, period is the wooden door which was used at his tomb. It shows that about A.D. 1000 in western Asia the Islamic art of carving was already on the same path which it was following under the Fatimids in Cairo. In book illumination the acquaintance with Hindu work proved a stimulus which found its outlet in the Baghdad school, while in the so-called Mosul ceramics we repeatedly come upon motifs which clearly derive from Buddhist models.

CHAPTER FIVE

The Persian Mongol Style

THE power of the Seljuks had pushed the Caliphate right into the background, but at least they had let it remain as a spiritual authority. The great Mongol invasion of the mid-13th century put an end, along with much else, to this remnant of past glories. Nomadic tribes from the Gobi desert had destroyed the might of China and now, led by the forceful Genghis Khan, they set out on a campaign of conquest of unequalled audacity to found a world empire. It embraced almost the whole Asiatic continent and at times penetrated deep into Europe. Hulagu, the grandson of the ruler of the world, had the last of the Abbasid Caliphs murdered in 1258 and founded his own dynasty as Il-Khan of Persia, while western Turkestan fell to the Shagatay line of the great Mongol imperial house. Both families reigned for about a century, and from the break-up of their domains Timur, who came to power in Transoxania in 1369, forged the last Asian world empire in history.

There are thus two consecutive periods, with a short interruption between them. In the first, the Il-Khan period, the Mongol element wrought changes in Persian art production, while in the second the art was already fully Iranized, and continued to develop into the 15th century as the Timurid style.

The great Mongol flood was no less than a disaster for the artistic activity of the Islamic Orient. But Hulagu and his successors came forward as generous patrons, and were earnestly and successfully concerned to bring their lands to a new flowering of culture. The dread Tamerlane (Timur) could not rest from his civilizing ambition until he had made his residence at Samarqand into the most splendid and grandiose metropolis of the Orient. He turned back to the ancient institution of public service (see p. 31) in order to assemble craftsmen from all his lands to work together on his buildings, and he gave new stimulus to the arts, without estranging them from their national individuality.

With the conquerors a stream of far Eastern motifs flooded over Persia and the neighbouring lands. The powerful new influences which poured in from a foreign world of imagination might have been expected, especially in times of political alliance with the Far East, to have risked swamping them with foreign ideas, had not the achievements of their previous development been too vital to let this be a real danger. We see, on the contrary, how Chinese patterns and fabulous animals very soon became stylized in the Islamic manner, fitting so easily into the native repertoire that the revolution in content pales before the continuity in form.

Funerary Building

The Seljuk form of tower was at first retained; the tomb of the daughters of Hulagu in Meragha, for instance, is entirely in the style of the mausolea of Nakhechevan. On the other hand the graves of the *imam* at Kum erected during this period stress the association with similar buildings in Iraq, referable to the common Shi'ite confession of the builders. In the domed mausolea we can see a new striving towards the monumental, which is best exemplified in the tomb of Uljaitu Khodabende (1304–1316) in Sultania, where he founded a temporary residence (plate 40b). The pointed cupola buttressed by eight pillars topped like minarets, shows a striking emphasis on the vertical. It has evoked comparisons with our Gothic system. In the Qubba-i-Sebs, a ruin in Kirman, this verticality was extended to the ribbed dome of the tower, and the new type thus evolved had considerable influence on the form in Timurid times.

Samarqand was given one of the world's most curious necropolises in the street of tombs of Shah Zinde. Several members of the family of the world conqueror are laid here; he himself had his tomb set back from it in the most splendid of these mausolea,

THE PERSIAN MONGOL STYLE

the famous Gur Emir (plate 39) built between 1490 and 1504.
It is a tower with a lower octagonal surround, a cylindrical drum,
a splendid fluted cupola with ribbon decoration rather like a tent,
and an *iwan* in front of it. The square of the inner room is rendered cross-shaped by niches roofed with stalactite vaulting. The
transition to the octagon is secured by a multiplication of squinch
niches; and over the 16-sided transitional zone stands the pointed
horseshoe cupola, under which lies a flat-vaulted crypt. The
imposing effect of both inside and out make the building
undoubtedly one of the most impressive monuments of Islamic
architecture.

Mosque and Madrasah

The type of mosque created by the Seljuks is represented in the
Friday mosque of Isfahan, but it did not find its ultimate form until the 14th century, with the four great *iwan* and the spacious
sanctuaries attached to them (fig 12). It established itself further in
Persia in the Mongol period and displaced everywhere the surviving hall buildings of earlier type. Thus the Feramin mosque of
1322 is a complex of vaulted pillared halls with an inserted cross,
formed of *iwan*: the main *iwan* has a dome chamber. In the Gauhar
Shad mosque in the sanctuary of the Imam Riza in Meshhed
(1418) visitors are particularly struck by the harmonious conson-
ance of all the different parts of the building.

Otherwise it was the pure domed mosque which grew increasingly dominant during the Timurid period, certainly influenced
by the harmony of proportions in the great mausolea. In Sunnite
buildings at least, it remained without a courtyard. The Kalyan
mosque in Bukhara is of this kind; it was built as a royal private
mosque with a tall entrance *iwan* and an impressive cylindrical
minaret. In Samarqand Timur built a great Friday mosque, which
according to surviving reports stood on stone pillars and had four
minarets placed at the corners. The Blue Mosque in Tebriz, of the
mid-15th century, was conceived entirely round a central point;
it now stands in ruins. The central domed hall was supported by
side chambers, and deepened by a vaulted tomb chamber (fig 16).
The Masjid-i-Shah in Meshhed of the year 1451 is reckoned to be

the work of the same architect. The dome is reached by a combination of squinches and pendentives on eight pillars.

The *madrasah* was not altered in any essentials during the time of the Hulagids. The Mirjaniya in Baghdad of the mid-14th century shows lecture halls, living rooms, *musalla* and a tomb chamber round the courtyard; the gate was originally flanked by two minarets and the central dome was raised on a drum. The institution was revived in Timurid times but there are unfortunately very few characteristic examples remaining, and most of those are

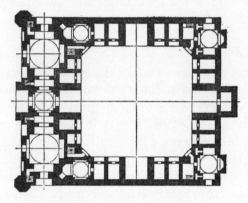

15. Ground plan of the Timurid *madrasah* in Khargird after Diez, *Churasanische Baudenkmäler*, pp. 72–76.)

badly damaged. The well-preserved *madrasah* in Khargird (near the Afghanistan border) was built by two architects from Shiraz, one of whom also built the Gauhar Shad mosque in Meshhed already mentioned and the Ulug Beg *madrasah* in Samarqand. A square courtyard is formed by four barrel-vaulted *iwan* with connecting arcades on two storeys (with corridors connecting the cells), and corner chambers (fig 15). The frontage consists of a vestibule formed by three dome chambers, and the high gateway with two round minarets at the corners. In Samarqand only formless ruins remain of the *madrasah* Bibi Hanum, planned by Timur himself in 1399. It treats the traditional ground plan for these college buildings in an interestingly freer manner, creating a rectangle of contiguous cells with towering domed halls and a gigantic portal arch in the middle of each façade. Very little remains either of Ulug Beg's *madrasah* (1447–1449) which was contained by four minarets; only the frontage of the entrance and the *iwan* opposite still stand. The two other law schools which now are combined with it to surround the impressive Rigistan Square are of later origin, though still true to Mongol tradition. This tradition continued in many other instances in Turkestan:

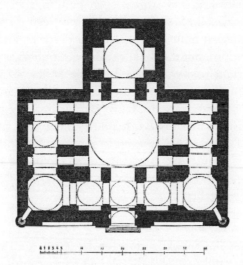

16. Ground plan of the 'Blue Mosque' in Tebriz (so called from the background colour of its exceptionally rich facing of faience mosaic) after P. Caste, *Monuments modernes de la Perse*, Paris, 1867. Cf. Sarre, *Denkmäler persischer Baukunst*.

two examples are the *madrasah* of Shir Dar of 1610 (plate 40a) with its deeply ribbed dome and a ground plan similar to Khargird, and the Tilla Kari; both have massive *iwan* gates beside which the two-storeyed street fronts seem excessively low, and cylindrical towers in the corners.

Secular Building

We have to turn to Marco Polo, who stayed at the court of Genghis Khan, for an idea of the residence of the great Mongol emperor in Karakorum. But this accurate description cannot help with the palaces which Hulagu and his successors built for themselves inside the Islamic countries, because they certainly used regional traditions. Neither in Baghdad, Tebriz nor in Sultania, the other residences of the Il-Khans, have any traces remained of sites of this kind. Even in Samarqand, which Timur raised to the status of a world capital at the end of the 14th century, and decked with splendid palaces, there is nothing to serve as definite evidence of what the earlier large secular buildings were like. It may be that the palace in Sesh (west Turkestan) can do something to fill the gap; it was built by the same emperor and occupied for a long time by him, but the details still await publication.

An important role was played on the Mongol imperial roads by post houses (*yam*). They were described by Marco Polo, and differed in several respects from caravanserai. An inscription proves the Khan Ortma in Baghdad to be one such; it was built in 1359, and is fortunately preserved to some extent, and now used as a Museum of Islamic Art. It consists of an elongated hall with ribbed vaulting, with two storeys of rooms round it, the upper ones connected by a gallery.

Architectural Decoration

Apart from the Seljuk stone portals which remained confined to Asia Minor and were not developed further until the Ottoman style was formed, techniques of decoration evolved during the earlier periods were improved during the Mongol period and brought to a most splendid climax of development.

Marble facings seem to have been used only exceptionally, for example on Timur's now vanished mosque in Samarqand. Stucco on the other hand was often applied and was especially liked for furnishing the prayer niches in mosques and mausolea. The Friday Mosque in Isfahan was given a richly decorated *mihrab* of stucco in 1310, with inscriptions and arabesques, and so was the mosque in Marand. From a few heads idealized in pure Mongol style we can deduce that in some palaces the figure sculpture in stucco introduced by the Seljuks lived on.

The greatest advance of this period is in the various ceramic techniques, which reached the height of perfection in every sphere. Even decoration in unglazed brick is shown to have progressed by the Kalyan minaret in Bukhara. It has large-scale close and richly varied horizontal patterning, and the surfaces are also animated by varied courses of glazed bricks. Mosaic with pieces of brick was still used, for example in Sultania; in the Timurid period it was universally replaced by the now highly perfected faience mosaic, most outstandingly exemplified in the Gur Emir, in the mosques of Meshhed and above all in the Blue Mosque of Tebriz, so-called from the luminous cobalt ground of its ceramic facing. The range of colours is considerably wider than at Konia: it includes blue, turquoise, white, yellow, green, brown, aubergine and black; the imperishable luminosity of these tones survives in the ruins of today to remind us of the splendour of façades, *iwan* and domes. The designs are wrought with astonishing delicacy, as though a miniaturist had applied them with his brush; the Persian potters seem to have made sport of the technical difficulties, cutting out and piecing together the tesserae so that the *élan* of drawing in friezes of inscriptions or fields of ornament is unbroken; in mosaics, man can do no more (cf. plate 40a).

Tiles were also harnessed to the service of outside decoration: either they were monochrome glazed tiles with motifs scratched on so that they stood out against the background colour, or, particularly on various buildings in Bukhara and Samarqand, they were deeply engraved with the design and then glazed, mostly green with some white and manganese brown; or else the colours were kept separate on smooth tiles by means of waxed cord technique. A few portals, like that at the mausoleum of Chojuk Bika, show clearly how the problem of 'overall surface covering' was solved by unbroken ceramic facing (plate 41).

In these methods of decoration the assistance of another feature was very important. This was the stalactite motif used increasingly on portal *iwan*, prayer niches, etc. It made possible in Persia, for example in the sanctuary of the Gauhar Shad mosque in Meshhed, the rich honeycombed vaults like those furnishing the Alhambra in 14th century Moorish style.

Lustred *mihrabs* and lustre tiles for wall coverings in star and cross shapes were not used after the period of the Il-Khans; the prayer niche of a mausoleum from Feramin is now in the University Museum of Philadelphia, and a series of tiles of like provenance, with arabesques and other plant motifs, some with the date 661 H (1262) are found in a number of collections. Some lustre facings in private houses had most charming figure designs, but even these went out of use in the early 14th century; in the Timurid period lustre seems to have been entirely abandoned, having been gradually superseded by polychrome tiles.

Mongol Ornament

In epigraphy the new epoch does not seem to have brought any notable additions to the great achievements reached under the Seljuks. The revolution in abstract and figurative decoration was all the greater and more incisive, in spite of tenacious adherence to tradition.

Of especial importance for further developments in the whole of western Asia was the introduction of a Chinese motif called the 'ling-chih', a fungus-like shape originally of symbolic significance and now in Persia and subject to the Islamic sense of stylization destined to a rich development as a cloud band. From this period onwards it becomes part of the basic stock-in-trade of all decorative techniques, and was specially valuable in relieving the now exhausted arabesque from its manifold ornamental duties. The adoption of the Chinese lotus flower was another important innovation, offering as it did an alternative to the palmette forms which were the other basic standby and also in need of refreshment; flower heads and many other plant forms were accepted as a welcome enrichment and employed with great skill.

More dubious was the effect of the assault of Far Eastern fabulous beasts. The unreality of their presentation must have appealed to the Islamic artist with his need to denaturalize animal forms, and he adopted them in large quantities, without any consideration of the symbolism which they might possess in China. They were, however, immediately modified to a Persian Islamic style, and many of them first received their characteristic impress here. Further, they were often brought into combinations which arose not from the Chinese, but from a specifically Persian world of imagination: following, confronting or attacking each other. In general all pictures of dragons, kilins (unicorn, lion or stag kilins *inter alia*), fung huang (phoenix) and such like were more interesting when they were known from the Chinese picture scrolls—collected, for example, by Timur—and the artists were able to add them painlessly to the traditional repertoire of motifs by providing the right ornamental backing. It is important to notice how they became naturalized into the repertoire, migrating to some extent too into India and Turkey. In the 16th century when a new national art style was forged in Persia they were no longer felt to be alien. The battle of the dragon with the phoenix, for example, is introduced in hundreds of variants, without being given any symbolic meaning, but simply because the designer enjoyed the decorative confrontation of fantastic animal forms.

Book Illumination and Painting

Baghdad in the Il-Khan period continued to hold the leading position in Koran illumination which it had held until then. It developed mainly the Naskhi hand into a decorative script for large books, which bear comparison with the old Kufic parchment Korans for weighty monumentality. The characters are scattered with gold, the verses set in scalloped cloud-panels and the backgrounds often filled in with decorative stem work (plate 42a). The title pages have a new embellishment, being broken up into different geometric fields filled with text and ornament. Towards the end of the 14th century Tebriz and Samarqand which were already famous for their books came to hold a leading position. The decoration is richer in colour and the ornament increasingly close on the surface of the pages, sometimes ousting the script entirely. Chapter heads and border medallions became increasingly sumptuous interruptions of the text, and book decoration assumed altogether a striking similarity to the faience mosaic of domes and *iwan*. In fact, of course, the illuminators were drawn into designing for ceramic facings, and used the style they had developed in their own craft for the patterns they prepared for ceramics.

In the Timurid period the art of binding began to flourish where previously only occasional examples of any magnificence had been made. It was primarily luxury manuscripts of secular works that encouraged the use of gold and blind tooling; they also evoked the refinement of the filigree-like cut leather on the inner cover. The binders soon became capable of handling the beloved Mongol animal motifs in this medium too.

Contact with the work of the Chinese Yüan masters inspired miniature painting to a fruitful and varied development such as could never have been foreseen from the products of the Baghdad school. This influence can be seen still at work in some animal pictures in one of the bestiaries of the late 13th century now preserved in the Morgan Library, and other pictures by the same hand also show Far Eastern features, some more strikingly than others (plate 43a). Illustrations of Mongolian historical works seem to show this contact very consistently (plate 43b); the *World Chronicle* of the vizir Rashid-ed-dir in the edition of 1307/13 preserved in London and Edinburgh is not only allied technically to Chinese ink painting style in its miniatures, but gives a purely Mongol character to the historical scenes in the costumes portrayed. It is, incidentally, the first time that the life and deeds of the Prophet Muhammad are pictured without any religious inhibition. It should be remembered that the Hulagids had Buddhist and Christian leanings, and were themselves only late converted to Islam, interpreting its precepts in a very liberal manner.

In other manuscripts we can follow step by step the penetration of the Far Eastern element both in landscape and figure compositions, how it sometimes breaks in vehemently and threatens to throw all tradition overboard, before it appears again subdued into the Islamic decorative style. Subsequently the painters were mainly in demand for luxury editions of the most popular Persian epics, and we soon see them vying with each other to invent effective compositions for the most important scenes from Firdusi's book of heroes, from Nizami's sentimental verses about Majnun and Leila or Khosrau and Shirin, and other texts in favour at the time (plate 44b). These are pictures in which the Chinese stimuli, in acting on the ancient Iranian vision, have led gradually to a fantastic and romantic representation of landscape. In the late 14th century it culminated in the surprising sunset glow of the

Baghdad school, and then was taken over by Shiraz and Herat, the centres of the future. The feeling of the Persian artist for the mysterious beauty of nature, for luxurious gardens and magical blossoms finds nostalgic expression here (plate 45). The residence in Khorasan assumes particular importance from the Academy for the Arts of the Book founded there by the Timurid prince Baisonqur. It was in many ways a fruitful influence.

In calligraphy the Nast'aliq script invented by Mir 'Ali established itself as the new Persian cursive writing. It found its most brilliant champion and practitioner in Sultan 'Ali of Meshhed. Its effect on paintings was stimulating both as to composition and colour, and more and more exquisite work resulted. Compositions were deliberately complicated by the placing of the verses, which were set down ahead and often laid out with wilful caprice for the miniatures to enclose: the intimate harmony of picture and text was the first concern of the art of the book. This postulation of unified surface effect combined with the example of the Far East prevented Persian book illuminators from using horizontal perspective to give depth to their pictures, such as was being evolved in the West. In Samarqand and in Bukhara it seems that fine brush drawing with fine touching up in gold was already in favour; later it spread into both the Persian and Indian schools of painting.

Carpets and Textiles

During the Mongol period the demand for carpets must have been met primarily by each tribe producing for itself. At any rate there is no evidence that a native industry flourished anywhere in Persia under the Hulagids. The industry founded by the Seljuks in Asia Minor continued its activity, and seems to have spread to the Armenian highlands and the Caucasus. This latter region is considered to be the homeland of a number of ancient knotted specimens which show their origination in the Mongol period because they introduce Mongol animal motifs. The oldest example of these has a repeat of the dragon fighting the phoenix in two compartments (originally certainly more). The motif is very tersely and heavily translated into the plain language of knotting, in a small number of harsh colours (plate 42b). The pattern is reproduced

in an Italian painting of about 1440, and other pictures of the
Florentine and Sienese schools prove that examples of Caucasian
or Anatolian animal rugs which have not themselves survived
were exported to Italy as early as the 14th century.

In a group which has survived in some numbers from the 15th
century, and out of which the so-called Kuba carpets later
developed, single dragons and pairs of fabulous beasts, often no
longer identifiable, are ranged over the field with palmettes and
other plant forms; they clearly anticipate the trend towards
'vegetablization' of the animal decoration which is immanent.
Technically these pieces signify a considerable advance in the
extraordinary richness of their forms and colours. The designs are
oriented along the length and have only narrow borders. They
have long been attributed to Armenia, and it has not yet been
proved that they were produced by Muslims, but their Caucasian
origin can hardly be questioned. In Persia itself purely abstract
medallion carpets were made from the 15th century, as we can
conclude from their appearance in Timurid miniatures. It is quite
likely that one or other of the surviving examples with rather stiff
scroll-work is as old as this, but the type flourished mainly in the
following period.

There was no need of the special circumstance of Mongol invasion to broadcast the patterns on Chinese silk in western Asia;
they had repeatedly found their way there even in times of peace,
ever since Late Classical times. But this time the fecundation was
especially lasting, and its most important effect was to bring about
improvements in the native products. Production of gold brocades after Chinese models came first; this was hardly established
before it brought about a parallel movement in Western manu-
factures, first and foremost in Venice and Lucca. The fine cloths
of the 13th and 14th centuries known as 'panni tartarici' probably
stemmed from Turkestan; they have been preserved as vestments
in various church treasures and recently came to light in the Scali-
ger graves in Verona; they have separate compartmemts with Far
Eastern fabulous animals still rendered quite faithfully like the
originals, but alongside them are decorative motifs in definitely
Islamic style, and Arabic inscriptions and even sometimes signatures.

The Timurid period next gave new textiles to Persia in the shape of gold and silver brocades in which rows of Far Eastern animals appear, singly over a background of wavy scrolls or else in pairs in ogival compartments. At first these were only lightly suggested but they gradually were more strongly defined and were to become typical of later developments. The centres in which these cloths were made have not yet been found for certain, but it is clear that a new sense of form entered Islamic workshops with the *kilins, fung huangs,* lotus flowers and the many other themes, at the same time as it was informing the Western silk industry.

Persian Mongol Metalwork and Faience

The bronze school of Mosul sent its scions to Baghdad and Persia, as has already been explained, yet as early as the Il-Khan period a slackening in technical finesse is apparent, in spite of the re-animation of decorative design which immediately made itself felt here also. The bodies of vessels are closely and bewilderingly covered with engraving, and the inlays become either sketchy or incomplete. Altogether the Timurid period offers nothing noteworthy in bronze work. On the other hand inlay on steel and iron raised weapon-making to a fine art, and the methods of incrustation used so far underwent many changes. The ribbed bell shape of helmet emerges, to be worn over the turban, with eye slits, the body of it decorated with inscriptions and flowered scrolls drawn in close lines of fine hammered-in silver wire (plate 44a). From this Mongol model then developed both the smaller, flatter Persian helmet and the conical Turkish head piece. Exceptionally there are helmets with a complete face piece, an outstanding example of which is in the Armoury in Moscow. The usual sword was not, as might be thought, the curved sabre, but was still the straight broad blade which often bore on its hilt the representation of the fight between dragon and phoenix over close leafy scrolls in beautiful gold inlay. The forms of shield and battle-axe later used by Persians and Turks were most likely already being made.

It is generally accepted that when Rayy was destroyed by the Mongols this important Persian ceramic centre went out of production; there is no evidence that the efforts of Hulagu and his successors to bring new workshops to life met with any success. The many surviving Persian faiences of the later 13th and 14th century cannot be associated with Rayy, while Kashan certainly carried on and developed several of the techniques and forms created there. This is true above all of lustre majolica; the potters still held mainly to Seljuk tradition for its themes, but handled them more lightly and loosely and, as on the tiles, emphasized them more strongly by relief.

We also have charming monochrome glazed wares from this phase, with incised and relief decoration, some decorated in black with transparent turquoise glaze, and lastly a new class with blue and black painting on a white ground; this type was the earliest to adopt the new style. These groups, mostly using lead glazes, are referred to Sultanabad, where many similar pieces have been excavated, but which has never seriously come into consideration as a place of manufacture. Ceramic ware of the Timurid period is little known; evidently the court, which, of course, used mainly Chinese porcelain, took little interest in its advancement.

CHAPTER SIX

Mamluk Art

THE forceful personality of Saladin found expression in more than one field of activity. He was of Kurdish extraction and reached distinction under the Zengid Nur ed-din. In 1171 he put an end to the Fatimid regime in Egypt and then extended his own, Ayyubid, dynasty into Syria and Arabia, destroying the kingdom of Jerusalem in 1187. But apart from his military victories his influence was brought to bear on cultural matters, and he led Egypt once more to the Sunnite confession and so into closer contact with her neighbours. He and his successors also directed the arts into new paths, though their rule lasted too short a time, and too few of their buildings have survived, for us now to ascribe to them more than an intermediary role between the Seljuk and Mamluk styles. The Seljuk style lived on in Syria under their sceptre, as we have already seen, their preference for figure motifs unaffected by their orthodoxy; in many ways the foundations for the Mamluk style were laid, although it did not come to full fruition until the new rulers were in power.

The Mamluks were originally white slaves of Turkish descent who rose to be leaders of mercenaries and at the right moment seized power, as the Seljuk Atabegs had done. They succeeded one another in quick, often violent, succession in two lines: the first, the Bahrits (1250–1390), a single dynasty; while the Borjits (1382–1517), who began with Sultan Barquq, were drawn from several Circassian families. Although many of them had to spend years in working gradually towards a position which they then only enjoyed for a short span they kept the country at a high level of culture. Between their battles with the crusaders, whom they finally defeated, and with the Mongols, against whose onslaughts their heroic defence twice saved the land of the Nile, they found time to embellish their capital with buildings and to guide their industries to achievements which were the admiration of the whole world. The Abbasids, who had been driven from Baghdad, and whose power had become merely ceremonial, continued their purely formal Caliphate under the protection of the Cairene court, their existence being suffered, of course, solely to add lustre to the effective ruler.

The Mamluk period is significant in the development of Islamic art particularly for the inclusion of Egypt into the Turkish stylistic sphere. This involved many revolutionary changes. But it will be seen from the following pages that Cairo did not of course sail untrammelled into the Turkish stream; rather did it adopt from there ideas of construction and ornament and combine them with the traditions preserved from the Fatimid period; nor did it shut itself off from either Moorish or Western inspiration. Cairo can rather be characterized as a centre where foreign architectural ideas were borrowed and fitted into the traditional cultural complex.

Mamluk Sacred Building

Saladin introduced the *madrasah* from Syria in its typical four-part lay-out, and the Mamluks themselves brought in the domed tomb from west Turkestan. Both these elements soon influenced the plan of the mosque, without entirely ousting the old pillared mosque with its traditional ground plan. It can still be seen applied, for example, in the mosque of Zahir Baybar (1260–1277), a square with salient gateways on three sides and emphasis on the central aisle on the *qibla* side achieved *inter alia* by a dome in front of the *mihrab*. Even the mosque of an-Nasir on the citadel (1318) belongs to this class, and the smaller one of Sultan al-Moayed (1416–1419); each of them has a tomb chamber at the side of the main *iwan*, and the *iwan* is designed as a pillared hall. Where the *madrasah* ground plan was adopted the function of the building was correspondingly enlarged, so that it could be used both as mosque and *madrasah*, as indeed it often is at the present day. This also happened with most of the tomb mosques, in which the founders were set on one side and the monastic or academic side was stressed. The main *iwan* with the *qibla*, and the hall facing it were developed and the other two *iwan* shrank into mere niche recesses. Under the Circassian Mamluks in the 15th century a new type of mosque was built with dimensions smaller by the elimination of the open court.

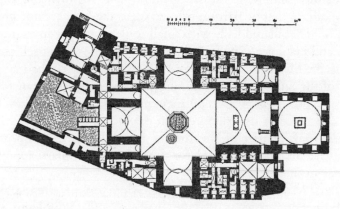

17. Ground plan of the tomb-*madrasah* of Sultan Hassan in Cairo (after J. Franz Pasha, *Die Baukunst des Islam*, Darmstadt, 1887; 1896 edition). The largest of the four different-sized *iwan* served as a mosque. The four corners have narrow multi-storeyed buildings of cubicles for the students.

The mausolea themselves, of which a few such as that of the Imam Shafi'i of 1211 go back to Ayyubid times, were uniform in plan. They show few changes in their main lines, which is surprising, particularly in later times when so many were built. The new style of building was certainly brought from Turkestan, but once in Egypt it developed in a definite manner. The helmet shape triumphed for the dome; it sat on the polygonal or round base achieved through spherical triangles often formed by a multiplication of stalactites, without any organic relation to the lower building. Cairo has a whole complex of these memorial buildings which may well lay claim to being the most picturesque necropolis in the world; this is the so-called Tombs of the Caliphs which lies spread across the desert landscape to the east of the town

(plate 47). Very few remain from the Bahrit period, and the similarity of the rest is astonishing; some are double tombs with twin
domes bound together by an *iwan* vaulting.

The form of the *Khanka* probably dates back to Saladin; it consists of cloisters with mosque, tomb, sometimes a fountain (*sebil*)
and school (*kuttab*). The Khanka of Baybar of 1310 has a madrasah
plan with courtyard cells and a tomb chapel; larger 15th century
sites of this kind with various ground plans stand in the Cairo
necropolis. In that of Barquq of 1400–1410 the *iwan* are not single
units, but are pillared halls with small rows of domes; in two corners stand mausolea. There is a large group in the town itself comprising the Moristan (hospital) of Qalaun (after 1284), the mausoleum of the Sultan and the mosque (plate 46); the Moristan, with
a dome on six piers and six pillars joined by horseshoe arches, has
been compared in its structure with the Dome of the Rock. The
hospital took in part of the former Fatimid palace; we possess
exhaustive descriptions of its, for those days, exemplary appointments.

In Syria Mamluk building kept quite close to the Cairene types;
the distinction between mosque, *madrasah* and mausoleum was
equally vague. Twin domes became frequent on the *turbe*,
separated by the alcove of the portal.

Style of Façades and Interior Decoration

As we have seen, a strong tendency to articulate the façade was
in existence as early as the Fatimid period in Egypt; now it dictated the style of the exterior and so influenced structural problems
in general. Stone came to be used almost exclusively for sacred
building, and pleasure in its manipulation was as important a factor as the desire for picturesque effects. The horizontal line was
stressed by alternating courses of yellow and dark red stone; these
were later often only a facing (e.g. in the chessboard patterning
on Qalaun's building). On door and window lintels the variety of
material was sometimes used to produce an attractive toothing.
The articulation itself was achieved by shallow niches with tall,
usually pointed arches, sometimes with an angular stalactite
moulding separating them, and pierced with windows, straight,

pointed or trefoil. As a rule the section of the building itself was then crowned with cresting. The pointed arch sometimes (e.g. in the Qalaun, plate 46) takes on quite a Western form, it must be under the influence of the Gothic introduced into Palestine by the crusaders. To make the vertical articulations more effective the tall narrow alcove of the gateway is usually placed in a corner of the façade instead of in the middle, with a raised threshold and steps. It is generally completed with a high trefoil arch, and behind it rises the stalactite vaulting which we have already met in Konia, suggesting that in general the style of façades in Cairo may have acquired something from Seljuk Asia Minor. Usually the buildings have several rows of windows and sometimes charming loggias at the corners. In the Madrasah of Sultan Hassan the street front is remarkably beautiful.

An important feature in the picturesque effect of these buildings is the inclusion of the minarets in the façade, in such a way that they rise at one corner, or both, starting straight from the parapet, without a plinth. Their elevation, now so typical of the Cairo scene, first square, then octagonal, then round, was anticipated in Fatimid times; but now was enlivened with the characteristic niches and stalactite galleries (plate 20a). The often lavish use of these motifs was combined with geometric ornament to produce manifold variations, not one of which failed, right through the period, in its elegance of proportions and fine sense of organic structure.

Contrast to the light, never excessively tall minarets was sought in heavier domes, to give a more impressive silhouette to religious edifices. It is indicative of this their function that their steep elegant curves are not designed for any requirement of the inner structure, which is in itself quite undemanding, but simply for the exterior effect. This was also served by vertical fluting, horizontal zigzags or even rich stone carving in star-shaped compartments with arabesques (e.g. in the tomb mosque of Qait Bey). The Mamluk architects had no thought of grandiose monumentality, and it did not occur to them, their successful efforts with pendentive construction notwithstanding, to take up the challenge of a gigantic dominating dome over a strictly centralized building complex. This problem was first tackled and solved by Ottoman architects.

In Cairo, however compact the plan, particularly in the larger tomb mosques, may be, we are always made aware that it is conceived as a combination of a number of separate buildings, both in ground plan and in dividing up the exterior, so that the whole appears as rather picturesque, and always very harmonious scenery.

The stalactite motif was much used inside, particularly on the pendentives, where it assumed some architectonic importance. Coloured marble slabs, and, particularly on the *mihrab* wall, stone mosaic, were used on the walls. The prayer niche was no longer, as in the Fatimid period, faced with stucco or wood, but was given an organic function; the round or pointed arch inside a rectangular frame had especially rich marble mosaic decoration, with geometric and curving patterns of great detail and delicacy (plate 48). Sometimes, for example in the Qalaun *madrasah*, there are galleries of round arches which may have been inspired by Romanesque buildings in Tuscany. The *minbar* was now usually made of marble, and so more intimately integrated into the building.

The flat-roofed *iwan* had their timbers gilded and painted with scrolls; and here, as in the domes, stucco friezes with decorative script and rich abstract ornament may still be met with. But ceramic inlay, as known in Persia and Asia Minor, was not usual. The doors were cased in bronze plaques fitted together in a style taken over from wood panelling. The stucco lattice windows with coloured glass (*qamriya*) which had already been made in the Fatimid period were now more richly appointed and designed with the most varied patterns; like the stained glass of the West they softened the daylight which now, with the increased number of openings, threatened to be too harsh.

Secular Building

Saladin had an ambitious plan for the fortification of Cairo, which in fact was never more than partially completed. The high citadel, which is essentially his work, was to be incorporated into the great town wall and so create a unified system of defence, with half-round towers instead of the Fatimid faceted ones, and a rectangular bend through the gateways. The Mamluks added little new.

At the time of the Napoleonic conquest remains of the Ayyubid residence in Cairo were still standing, and they were then surveyed. Among them was a large reception hall surrounded by pillared porticoes and roofed with a dome raised on massive stalactite pendentives. Of the Mamluk palaces only the Dar Beshtak of 1339 and that of Qait Bey survive. The latter, of which very little is preserved, is typical of the noble Cairenc dwelling house since the 15th century. It regularly has an upper storey that served as the *harim* with a great hall (*qaʻa*) which opened in a loggia over the inner courtyard. Downstairs the reception room (*mandara*) lay along the courtyard. The *qaʻa* consisted of three parts, the central one generally deeper than the side *iwan*, and usually with a water basin and fountain. It was generally roofed with a cupola perforated with *qamirya* (see above). The marble facings, and the shapes of arches and capitals are the same as in sacred buildings; for the inner fittings more use was made of carved, painted and panelled wood here than in religious buildings, and brick was more used than stone as building material. Extensive use of floor mosaic was important for the development of geometric patterns of all kinds, both in Egypt and Syria.

In Syria, both in Aleppo and Damascus, there was also usually a three-part *qaʻa*, but it was T-shaped, clearly deriving from older native traditions. It was very richly decked with stone mosaic and panelling and it continued thus into later times. The earliest surviving examples are all of the Ottoman period.

Among secular buildings the caravanserai and warehouses (*okel*) were of architectural note; two remain from the time of Qait Bey in Cairo, one with a splendid stalactite portal, the other, erected near Bab en-Nasr in 1468, with a large inner courtyard and an imposing four-storeyed façade. Other examples remain in the Nile delta and in Syria; among the latter the stately Khan Vezir in Aleppo is late, but still in strictly Mamluk form with many charming details.

The streets of Cairo even today are characterized by the bow-shaped wooden lattices (*mashrabiye*) in the projecting upper storeys. The older examples are sometimes deserving of attention for their turnery as much as are the brackets on which they rest for their carving. They allowed the women to watch the life of the streets and squares without themselves being seen.

Epigraphy, Heraldry and Abstract Ornament

The new epoch introduced a revolution in epigraphic decoration. The graceful vertical hand based on Fatimid Kufic was still practised and sometimes as richly exploited as in Persia, but the characteristic note of Mamluk epigraphy is given by the round Naskhi hand introduced by the Ayyubids, in the form mainly restricted to Egypt and Syria. It is distinguished by its especially tall format. This variant, which provided equally lapidary effects to the Kufic, is found in building inscriptions and in the epigraphy on vessels, where it generally dominates all other elements of decoration.

A favourite device was to interrupt friezes of script with round or oval medallions containing heraldic motifs. These are the 'speaking' emblems of the different court functionaries (cup-bearer, private secretary, master of polo, sword bearer, wardrobe master, chess master, cavalry commander, archery commander, etc) which were commonly used under the Ayyubids and even more under the Mamluks. In some cases they may have acquired the significance of family emblems with the heredity of the office; at any rate they are a sure criterion for dating the art of this period (cf. plate 49b).

Beside these two elements geometric and plant motifs still played an essential part in the decoration of objects. New types were created here, too, either contained in medallions, rosettes and cartouches or covering the surface in a continuous band of pattern. Due partly to Mongol influence naturalistic flowers (lotus flowers, inter alia) were added to the manifold arabesque and palmette representations, while animal motifs, even the harmless ornamental processions of animals, had increasingly to give way under the strict Sunnite regulation.

Mamluk Mosque Furniture

Perhaps in no other period of Islamic art has the demand for ceremonial cult objects for mosques, madrasah and mausolea so

influenced the general style of utensils as in the Mamluk era. The
return to Sunnite orthodoxy, bringing at last a complete renunci-
ation of figurative ornament, and the consciousness that it was
still possible to create fine work even inside this voluntarily accepted
restriction seems to have spurred on patrons to give costly commissions and craftsmen to produce outstanding work.

The most important piece of furniture was the pulpit; and despite its constant form, new technical and ornamental ideas were
always being found for it. It introduced further innovations even
now into wood carving, which then gradually spread to doors,
ceilings and window shutters. A framework of sunk panels usually
divided the surfaces into irregular fields, which were filled with
separate carved designs of various sizes in the same or different
woods, bone or ivory. This opened up the development towards
true intarsia with a great variety of materials. As early as the 14th
century it led to the production of hexagonal tables (*kursi*) and
four-sided cases to hold the Koran. These objects were more often
made of bronze and here the technique of inlay came into its own.
It spread from Mesopotamia in the 13th century and reached as
far as Egypt. We know of craftsmen from Mosul and Baghdad
who settled at that time in Cairo, and soon the new technique of
gold and silver inlay was disseminated throughout the workshops
of the city. Particularly brilliant examples of this are the *kursi* of
Sultan Qalaun and a *kursi* of Sultan en-Nasir dated 1327 in the
Islamic Museum in Cairo (plate 50), and there are also a few large
Koran boxes preserved there. Apart from these the most important mosque furniture was candlesticks: two stately ones generally
stood near the *mihrab* and these were often richly ornamented.
Hanging lamps on the other hand were not as a rule inlaid but
sometimes engraved and now and then cut in *ajourée* with script
and abstract patterns. Usually at that time they were faceted in
shape, tapering towards the top and domed. Jugs were not needed
except in a humble capacity for washing before prayer, but ablution basins and water containers with saucers were often carved
from marble and adorned with arabesques and inscriptions (plate
49a).

One of the particular charms of Cairene mosques at that time were the costly enamelled and gilded glass hanging lamps regularly commissioned by Mamluk sultans or emirs. Like the drinking vessels before them, they were made in Syrian workshops, mainly in Aleppo. They vary little, some slenderer, some more squat, in the vase shape with swollen belly, broad neck, and glass rings for the chains; the light itself was in a funnel-shaped glass filled with oil and set inside. The decoration might be, as in other pieces of the period, heraldic shields and ornaments of the most varied styles and detail (plate 49b), or inscriptions including quotations from the Koran, blessings on the reigning Sultan, praises of the high-born patron. In later pieces plant ornament becomes rampant, and so dense that it makes the glass body almost invisible.

The main item in a pious endowment was of course in most cases a presentation luxury copy of the Koran. First of all it must be by the hand of a famous calligrapher, and Cairo had world-famous masters to boast of, particularly in the script much in favour at that time, an elegant derivative of Naskhi called *thuluth*. The illuminators entrusted with the painting and gilding of title pages, chapter headings and border medallions were adept at bringing variety into the schematized rigour of their predominantly blue and gold designs; the binders too manipulated the typically Mamluk blind tooling with extraordinary virtuosity (plate 51a). In the later phase they enlivened this technique with cut-out arabesque medallions over a silk ground. The large format Korans which make such an impressive collection in the National Library in Cairo show the Mamluk book artists as unrivalled in their respective crafts.

Mamluk Domestic Furnishing

Many of the objects used in places of worship which never had any liturgical significance might equally well be used in private houses. There is, for example, no question but that the *kursi* commissioned in several mosques were first in fashion in aristocratic households as serving tables for placing trays and dishes. Later also they were used in this way in Egypt and Syria. The original purpose of marble basins is difficult to guess at, nor can it often be decided whether the candlesticks served religious or secular ends, since the Koranic texts have nothing to offer by way of evidence. We are, however, certain of the use made of the handled jugs well known from this period for their well-proportioned elegance: like the silver-inlaid basins, dishes, trays and bowls (plate 51b), they were tableware; writing things, boxes and caskets were produced in the same technique also, mostly in Syrian workshops.

In Syria too was evolved the shape of the perforated silver-inlaid incense globes especially popular in Venice, where in the 14th and 15th centuries a whole guild of oriental craftsmen made bronze pieces all'azzimina (in the Persian style) and alla damaschina with silver inlay.

The so-called Fostat pottery found in the rubbish heaps of Old Cairo allows us to distinguish a few of the more ordinary wares which were doubtless produced in Egypt itself. Apparently the production of lustre wares had completely stopped, for the sherds of such luxury majolica as were found there are all patently Spanish imports. But there is a large number of bases of bowls of blue-and-white ware with many potters' signatures which prove that potters were brought here from Syria and Persia to revitalize the craft. Then the typical Mamluk ware with enamel glazes, mainly in yellow, brown and green tones, and scratched decoration is most important: it had inscriptions, emblems, vine scrolls and other plant motifs, but as well very lively drawings of animals and human figures (horsemen, huntsmen, etc); occasionally there are even modellings in the round. Lamps are found in many different shapes and styles, though mostly with simple glazes. Syria was as fruitful as Egypt in ceramic production and still produced outstanding faiences during the Mamluk period, combining the good technical tradition of the previous period with a fine understanding of decorative requirements.

The objects just described were given suitable display in the recessed cupboards built into the walls of the qa'a both in Egypt and Syria. These were furnished with openings of varying sizes and shapes in which each piece could be placed on its own; they are still preserved in the older houses in Cairo and Damascus and continued in fashion after the end of the period.

From the reports of early travellers it is clear that even late in the

Mamluk period knotted carpets were being made in Cairo for domestic use, and it may now be confidently accepted as proven that the so-called Damascus rugs, which wrongly bore this name in the Venetian market, are to be recognized as Egyptian. They survive in large numbers, some still belonging to the late 15th, some to the early 16th century, and all with one and the same three-colour scheme of cherry red, turquoise and emerald green. In their design they are unique: a bewildering mass of kaleidoscopically changing geometric compartments with plant pattern fillings covers the whole field, which is hardly to be distinguished from the border executed in the same colours. The material is a shiny wool, or exceptionally silk, and the rugs are either square— hence destined for the qa'a—or elongated. The finest example of this type came to the Austrian Kunstgewerbemuseum in Vienna from the Hapsburg Imperial house; it is all in silk, with minute detail combined in larger units, making a fascinating effect that changes with each direction of the light.

Enough examples of arms and armour remain to show that the same style of inlay was used for helmets and other pieces of armour as for bronze utensils. Magnificent examples have reached the Istanbul weapon collections. The famous Mamluk battle axes are especially tasteful both in blade and handle, certainly the most beautiful that Islamic weapon craft ever produced.

Textiles and Embroidery

The Tiraz organization which dominated the Fatimid period did not continue under the Mamluks. Its end brought the end of the technique of silk tapestry weave on linen. The new period is characterized primarily by the foundation of a new style of silk working, stimulated by the Chinese fabrics of the Mongol period. Trade relations with the Empire of the Golden Horde and with east Asia were lively, and we possess, among other examples, brocades which can be proved to have been produced there for the Cairene court (plate 52). They stimulated the development of Egyptian gold brocade technique, to which we owe a large number of the most magnificent vestments in early Church treasures; the cloths were thus clearly much prized in the West. Technically the relief effect puts them entirely in the same category as the Persian work of the same period (mainly 14th century), but they also show typical Mamluk features in the inclusion of unmistakable Far Eastern models in the drawing of the flowers and animals.

The foreign element is even more pronounced in the damasks (*kamkha*) made in Egypt and again much exported to Europe. The wavy scrolls, lotus palmettes, interlacery all derive from China and demonstrate the path by which such motifs penetrated to the generality of Mamluk decorative art. Besides these there are multicoloured, lighter silk weaves with confronted animals in ogival compartments and similar motifs which are to be recognized as work of this period and, indeed, have marginal inscriptions to prove it.

Linen was still much used for clothing, but was now preferred embroidered with silk. The outlining stem stitch had already been used in the Fatimid period, but now the usual practice was a most careful weaving stitch which imitated mechanically produced textiles to the point of deception. The patterns are given a harder contour than in weaving, and many of the motifs which were disseminated at this time found their way into Slavonic and Scandinavian folk art, where they have lived on for centuries in small-scale variants. Several samplers are known from this period. With them the soft outline of the so-called Holbein stitch came to Europe, to which we owe very charming Renaissance embroideries. Lastly, in the Mamluk period the usually monochrome block print on linen was popular; we even possess a number of the wood blocks which were used so skilfully that a very compact continuous design could be produced from them.

CHAPTER SEVEN

The Moorish Style

THE term Hispano-Mauresque is generally taken to include all the artistic activity of the Islamic West; it is more correct to distinguish Hispano-Arabic or Hispano-Umayyad from a truly Moorish period. This began with the dominance of the Mauretanian Berbers in the political sphere, which soon drove the purely Arab element into the background.

Andalusia held undisputed cultural sway during the Umayyad period, but she relinquished it to Morocco when the political changes occurred which united Spain and North Africa under the Almoravids towards the end of the 11th century. The puritanism of the Moorish military monks was carried abroad by them from their Saharan monasteries; it brought a salutary sobriety to an artistic taste run completely wild with ornamental excesses. After a short period of stagnation and self-analysis we see the first fruits of a new style in the mid-12th century under the Berber Almohad dynasty. It developed richly everywhere, and reached its perfection in 14th century Granada, the last bulwark of Islam in Spain where all energies were once more concentrated to create the Alhambra. The Merinids gave the new style its full expression in Fez and Tlemcen, for which they had long struggled from their garrison town al Mansura. In Tunis at the same time the Hafsids took it up, but with some reserve.

Morocco has remained true, right to the present day, to the traditions of this period, during which almost all her Islamic monuments were built; and whereas Algeria came under strong Turkish and European influence in the Corsair period during and after the 16th century, Tunisia was better able to protect herself. At all events the late 15th century saw the end of any development of the Moorish style even in North Africa, and all that remained was an unproductive aftermath with an occasional revival of traditional forms.

The new art style was adopted over the whole of Spain and North Africa, but although this region is so extensive, very few regional individualities emerged. Architects and craftsmen disseminated new ideas and forms everywhere at the same time, and just as Marrakesh and Seville entirely complement each other in the 12th century, so do Granada and Fez in the 14th. On the other hand the gulf separating the Islamic West from the other Muslim countries grew if possible wider still, and however much the technical ideas of Persia or Egypt were taken up they were immediately employed in the Mahgreb style. Thus this period in Islamic artistic creation is especially consistent and harmonious.

Sacred Building

The new period made virtually no change in the ground plan of the mosque as it had been built at Qairawan and Cordova. This is demonstrated by the ideal Moorish plan as it was realized in the sensitively conceived mosque of Mansura. The courtyard plan remained the rule, with either a short or an elongated flat-roofed hall of prayer and the higher and wider central nave running up to the *mihrab*. Almost always the other aisles ran perpendicular to the *qibla* wall; only exceptionally the arches joined parallel to the prayer wall and occasionally they joined in both directions (Qarawiyin mosque in Fez). Usually, again, the minaret stood in the centre of the opposite side of the court (*inter alia* in Mansura and in the Hassan mosque in Rabat), though it is sometimes moved from its ideal axis into one of the corners of the courtyard; unique is the early Tinmal which has the minaret rising directly over the *mihrab*.

The change in the system of supports is important. Columns are no longer used, but pillars of brick with angled profile and sometimes (e.g. in the Kutubiya in Marrakesh) with engaged half columns. The horse-shoe arches, with smooth or scalloped outline and for the most part slightly pointed at the top, begin low and so give the sanctuary an air of solemn weight (plate 53a); in the Almohad period a distinctive shape of pointed arch was introduced. In the period of the Alhambra the stilted round arch on columns which had been developing in palace architecture was introduced into mosque building, though examples of this have not survived at all in Spain. The arches are always kept in the rectangular frame (rab'a, Spanish arabá), and in the later phase they are often simply modelled inside this scaffolding in stucco, as is suitable to their purely decorative function.

The minarets were often built of stone, even on brick buildings, and at this time evolved the slender well-composed design which was to remain that of the Mahgreb henceforth. Their shape hardly altered; they still kept to the quadrilateral lower section with a ring of cresting, and a smaller superstructure of similar shape also with its crenellation, which is best preserved on the Kutubiya in Marrakesh. The surfaces are pierced by single or paired windows. The Giralda in Seville, once the tower of the Great Mosque, was much altered in its upper section, but at least we possess a faithful representation of it from the 16th century (plate 54). From the Almoravid period onwards the *mihrab* dome was constructed over stalactite squinches in a ribbed vaulting which far exceeded the beginnings made in Cordova, and it was given a crowning lantern; then in Granada the honeycomb vaulting was developed further (see below). The function of the main portals now became considerable: richly decorated and protected by a projecting wooden roof they give strong emphasis to the effect of the façade.

Like Saladin in Egypt, his contemporary Almohad Yaqub el-Mansur (1184–1199) introduced the *madrasah* into Spain and the Mahgreb, though there was a difference, in that here it was only the institution itself that counted, without any definite architectural ideas accompanying it. In fact this new type of religious building had no significance for architectural evolution in the Islamic West and exercised no influence of any sort on the plan of the mosque either; this not even in Fez, where the aspect of the city is dominated by the many 14th century *madrasah* commissioned and richly endowed by the Merinids.

The plan always arose entirely from the practical need to group round an open court a number of dwelling cells for the students and a lecture hall which had also to serve as a sanctuary, and the recollection of similar arrangements already met with in the older ribat (see p. 41) may also be partly to blame for the relaxed planning and the failure of any ideas of centralization to make progress. Perhaps they might have bethought themselves of uniting the four rites under one roof as in the Mustansiriya in Baghdad, had the occasion arisen; but the Malechite sect was so exclusive that it precluded any such situation. They were content as a rule to erect two-storeyed buildings round a rectangular court, at the narrow end of which, sometimes divided off by piers, lay a square or elongated lecture hall with the *mihrab*. Some *madrasah* were associated with nearby mosques, others were entirely independent buildings possessing even their own minarets. With all of them the main artistic importance lies in their decoration.

The Zawiya has some connection with these colleges. This served the monastic education or the devotions of some pious brotherhood and was generally erected at the tomb of a holy man. Very few old sites of this kind are known that have any artistic importance; they sometimes include *madrasah*, inn and mausoleum in a larger unit similar to the Mamluk *khanka*. The holy tomb itself (*qubba*), shining in blinding whiteness from the heights and penetrating the mystic darkness of woods and groves is an inseparable part of the North African landscape. These domed structures cluster round the town gates and particularly in cemeteries. They take on many shapes, but are always of modest proportions and never attain to architectural significance. They are, in fact, mostly of recent date, but the primitive form of vaulting shows that traditions which are centuries old have been tenaciously preserved. Most often the simple half dome stands over its square base; sometimes it has a roofing, or is conical in shape, or again it has a drum as a transitional section; in other cases the base is not shut in, but open with horseshoe arches. At larger sites an arcaded court lies in front of the tomb chamber.

Most of the mausolea of the princes were probably built in a

9

similar manner, except that they would be rather more monumental and, of course, the advances made in dome building on the
mosques were also used on them. Next to nothing remains of the
raudha of the kings of Granada, and only shapeless ruins of the
tombs of the Merinids near Fez; the earliest site of this character is
the 16th–17th century necropolis of the Sa'adites in Marrakesh,
with an oratorium and several tomb chambers. In rarer cases
whole tomb-mosques were founded, like those of the Mamluks in
Cairo. The ruins of one of these are preserved in Shella near
Rabat, founded in 1286 and completed in 1339 by the Merinid
Abu'l Hassan. The precinct is contained in a rectangle and includes two mosques, each with its own court and tower, three
tomb chambers and a garden; the arrangement of these elements
is picturesque rather than ordered.

Military Building

The example of their Saharan monasteries can have been of
little avail for permanent defensive buildings in the rawer climate
of the regions conquered by the Almoravids: it is not surprising
that very little remains of their fortifications. Under the Almohads a new concept of town walls and citadels (*qasba*) arose, and
this set the style for the whole period. Pisé supplanted dressed
stone; round towers gradually were replaced by angular ones, and
the gatehouses won especial importance both from the defensive
and the decorative point of view. The flanking towers were included in the imposing effect and even were often used to carry
decoration; the arch is always kept very heavy, mostly a slightly
pointed horseshoe.

The town walls of Tlemcen, old Fez and Marrakesh are basically Almohad; in Rabat, as the name implies, the town fortifications grew out of the castle of a military holy order, which was
later supplanted by the *qasba* of the Udaya. Two massive gatehouses with domed vestibules are here very well preserved, and
in Marrakesh there is the impressive 12th century Bab Agenau
with its stepped friezes of arcading round the low gate in its rectangular setting, with fillings of arabesques in the spandrels and a
framing of epigraphy (plate 53b). The Sun Gate in Toledo goes

back to the end of the 11th century, but was substantially restored later. In Seville there still stand a portion of the town wall built in 1221 and the now isolated 'Torre del Oro', twelve-sided with a smaller superstructure, evidently belonging to it as well. The best preserved Almohad fortress, though somewhat altered after its capture by the Christians in the 13th century, is Alcalá de Guadaira, which protected the road to Seville. The high main wall with its strong towers surrounds a donjon and has a lower protecting wall of its own. The extension of the *qasba* (Alcazaba) on the Alhambra is also of this period; in the 14th century it was drawn into the system of the royal palace built nearby, which itself looks from the outside exactly like a fortified castle precinct.

Morocco owes the walls of New Fez and of Shella near Rabat to the Merinids; opposite, in Salê, the infamous pirate harbour, a wharf was built above the river's mouth from which vessels reached the sea through the strongly protected Bab el-Mrisa. The most interesting fortification of this dynasty, however, was without doubt the garrison town of Mahallat al-Mansura, which was built before the gates of Tlemcen between 1298 and 1302 so as to force the latter to surrender by a complete siege; within the massive walls the great mosque and a stately palace were erected.

Palaces and Functional Buildings

The asceticism which distinguished the pious Almoravids forbade the construction of splendid palaces, and it is indicative that they gave the democratic name of Dar el-Umma (Peoples' House) to their residence in Marrakesh. They paid more attention to assuring their immortality by religious building than to their own personal comfort, and the Arab authors who are usually so loquacious on these matters have nothing precise to say of the palaces of this mighty dynasty. All that has survived is a few fragments of the residence of the Almohads in Seville, where they came to light adjoining the present Alcazar; but they consist of nothing but a few arches with sparsely decorated stucco.

Our earliest example of a Moorish royal palace is the world-famous 14th century Alhambra on the hill dominating Granada, built beside the older fortress (Alcazaba). It is mainly the work of

Yusuf I (1333–1353) and Muhammad V (1353–1391), but unfortunately it also is partly destroyed or replaced by later work. However, the articulation of the plan into three units remains clear (fig 18): 1. The *Meshwar* open to all, in which the Sultan dispensed justice and received the homage of his subjects; 2. the *Diwan* for festive and formal occasions and receptions with its throne room; 3. the *Harim* with the more intimate rooms of the prince. The low-sited 'patio de Mexuar' still recalls its original purpose, providing a room for the judge and a small oratorium.

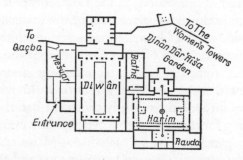

18. The sketch given here shows only the three main building complexes of the Alhambra palace. For a more detailed plan cf. in L. Torres Balbás, *Arte Ahmohade, Nazarí, Mudejar in Ars Hispaniae*, IV, 1949, fig 76.

The centre of the official area was formed by the great 'Myrtle Court' with its water basin and the Hall of Envoys built into the strong Komurish tower; attached to it was the Lion Court with its fountain, the centre of the *harim*. Two decorative pavilions project into it on the narrower sides, and domed rooms and longer halls surround it on all four sides. To the north one came to baths and gardens, to the east to smaller palaces and isolated dwelling towers for members of the royal family, to the south to the royal vault and palace mosque on the site of which a Christian church now stands. A further complex of buildings on the south of the Myrtle Court had to yield place in the 16th century to the palace of Charles V. From outside the Alhambra with its towered surrounding wall looks like a stern and heavy castle, giving no hint of the light gaiety of the interior.

The general plan of the Alhambra arose very much haphazard;

the strictly thought-out ground plans of the Abbasids are unknown in the Moorish territories. Palaces, too, show less concern with solid construction than with richness of decoration and ease and comfort, and often new structures were improvised and added as the need arose. Thus it is not surprising that most of them perished or were replaced after a short time. Of the pleasure palaces of the kings of Granada the Generalife Jenan el-'arif (architect's garden) built in 1339 still survives in part; here an elongated narrow water tank formed the centre of the plan. But the Alcazar in Seville, begun by Peter the Cruel in 1360 with the help of craftsmen from Granada, belongs already to the *mudejar*, the Moorish style which was carried on under Christian rule. Here too the tripartite arrangement seen in the Alhambra was observed: the Maidens' Court with the envoys' hall corresponded to the *Diwan*, and the Dolls' Court with its adjoining rooms to the *harim* (plate 58).

In Morocco the Merinid residences, which would have been so valuable in supplementing our knowledge of the Alhambra, have not survived. Only in the ruins of Mansura is it possible to recognize the site of two water basins like the one in the Myrtle Court; they belonged to the Victory Palace (Dar el-Fath) built by Abu'l Hassan in 1344 in the garrison town. Even the reputedly very magnificent palaces of the Hafsids in Tunis we only know from descriptions. A plan of 1622 of the Sultan's palace in Fez shows that then the *harim* court had two pavilions like the Alhambra and in the centre a long basin like that in the Generalife. Nothing but ruins remain of the extensive Badi', founded in the late 16th century in Marrakesh. It contained various water basins and domed pavilions; nor does anything more remain at Meknes of the gigantic residence of Mulay Isma'il, the last great building lord of the Mahgreb.

Bath buildings (*hammam*), examples of which remain in Spain from the Umayyad period and from the 11th to 13th centuries, always show close similarities to the Roman *thermae*. The main hall corresponding to the *apodyterium* had as a rule raised alcoves for reclining arranged round a dome on free-standing columns; *tepidarium* and *calidarium* were barrel vaulted, with small apertures to let in the light. Public fountains were at various times much favoured as charitable benefactions, but hardly attained to architectural importance. Marrakesh in particular has examples of great decorative charm. Among the hospitals (*moristan*) one erected by Yaqub el-Mansur in Marrakesh was much celebrated for its size and for both its artistic and hygienic appointments; like a similar building of Muhammad V in Granada, which later served as a mint (*zeca*), it is unfortunately destroyed.

Bazaars (*suq*, *qaisariya*) usually stood in most towns in a separate trading quarter in the vicinity of the main mosque. Parts belonging to the 13th–14th centuries are preserved in Tunis, with long brick barrel vaults on light columns, and in Granada a few 15th century arcades from the silk market are still standing, but are now walled up. Skilled restoration has made interesting architectural effects out of the rather neglected former corn exchange (*alhóndiga*, later 'Casa del Carbon') which was designed like the multi-storeyed warehouses (*fonduq*) with an inner courtyard. Other examples of older *fonduq* exist in Fez, among other places. Like the caravanserai in the Orient they served travelling merchants as inns at the same time.

Almohad Decoration

In the few surviving buildings of the Almoravid period their sobriety of decoration stands out against the oppressive excesses of late Umayyad style, but it was limited to purification, and introduced no new ideas. The prayer niche of the Great Mosque in Tlemcen, for example (c. 1135), gives no hint of approaching change, nor is there any suggestion of it in the stucco decoration of the *mihrab* at the Tunisian oasis of Tozeur, erected in 1194 by the last adherents of the Almoravids who were dispersed in the desert.

The great Almohad leader, Abdelmumen, is himself to be seen as the protagonist of the new trend which is found fully developed in the mosques of the mid-12th century built by him in Marrakesh and Tinmal. Stucco ornament dominates the brick structure everywhere, but it is under strict architectural control. It repeats in scalloped archivolts the shape of the horseshoe arch and articulates the surfaces into geometric frames, without filling them in with detail. It makes a sort of lacy valance like fine fretwork over the brick structure of the pointed arches and gives a rich stalactite moulding to the vaulting which is the triumph of its existence in Moorish art. The remnant of the Almohad palace in Seville and the former Synagogue in Toledo (plate 55) show how the 'Moorish' style from Morocco spread throughout Spain; the mighty gates of Marrakesh and Rabat (plate 53b) gave it a new sphere of development at the end of the 12th century by translating it into stone. The spandrels are filled with flat arabesques, and thus the field is open once again for abstract scrollwork, though in a new formulation. There appears here too for the first time a moulded motif which later was to have decisive importance as the stalactite frieze.

The Almohad *mihrab* is excellently exemplified in Tinmal. The horseshoe recess is plain and distinguished in effect in the setting of a rich and elegantly worked ornamental frame.

A further important step was being taken at the same time in the decoration of the minaret. The blind arcading was enriched into large fields of latticing in the style of brick patterning, and developed along the same lines as the contemporary Seljuk buildings of western Asia. The Giralda in Seville in its original condition (plate 54) is an excellent example of this. Painting was also sometimes used to enliven the ornament, for example in the Kutubiya. Lastly in epigraphy the lightly ornamented Kufic hand still held exclusive sway, and in the adornment of vessels a certain economy of decoration is to be noticed.

The Alhambra Style

While in the Almohad period the decoration is still held subject to structural ideas, in the 14th century these latter come completely under the dictates of the ornament. It is not quite certain that this decisive revolution took place in the royal castle at Granada itself, but since we know that craftsmen from there were called to Seville, Fez, Tlemcen and other residences, and the style of the surviving monuments shows a consistent connection, we have every reason to attribute the originating inspiration to the Alhambra and to name the style after it; unfortunately conclusive evidence is lost with the destruction of the earlier parts which dated from the late 13th and early 14th century.

The importance of the famous Moorish castle in architectural history lies not in the ground plan nor yet in the elevation, but in its ornament, which was primarily concerned with a functional articulation of the decorated surfaces and with the achievement of effects of perspective. The extraordinary technical skill with which stucco was now handled gave rise to the most daring experiments, and in the architectonic scenery of the Lion Court (plate 56) it achieved a truly theatrical effect. Marble columns of extreme delicacy are used, but either they are placed with their elegant round arches in a solid frame covered with plaster ornament and without any bearing function, or the load is so reduced by piercing the stucco that its pressure is easily supported. The daring moulded arches and stalactite domes are also modelled on to reasonable armatures; the boldness of the honeycomb corbelling breaks all bounds in the star vaulting of the Sisters' and Abencerrag halls (plate 57) where it is impossible to realize that they hang from a solid system of beams.

Surfaces were now all covered with continuous ornament, but all the patterns seem confined within frames, borders, friezes and fillings. Indoors the walls of rooms are covered from top to bottom with stucco panels, whose mechanical production enabled the work to be done quite quickly; only the dadoes are faced with faience mosaic. On the façades, galleries etc the fragile decoration is protected by projecting tiled wooden roofs.

In epigraphy the round Naskhi was combined with the vertical Kufic, made as complicated as possible with knots and curves, just as was happening in Persia and Egypt, but with a particular style in the formation of the curves. Among geometric motifs the lozenge lattice, known from Almohad minarets, was now favoured for the piercing of free-standing stucco walls; with it were used all possible star and ribbon combinations such as were dominating the ceramic field. Lastly in plant subjects the arabesque prevailed absolutely, recurring incessantly with inexhaustible variety alone, on stems or in bunches, in trefoils, palmettes or rosettes. Even the capitals are arabesqued and the friezes of inscription are embedded in a maze of split leaf scrolls. The ever-recurring emblem of the kings of Granada, with the device 'No victor but God' is the only heraldic motif in the Islamic West. As on the Lion fountain, which gave its name to the *harim* courtyard, a freer decorative sculpture may occasionally have come into service.

Apart from what was created in the Alhambra there is very little new in the decoration of the Merinid buildings in North Africa. Their value to us lies in the fact that they are mostly religious and so can suggest what the similar buildings, now destroyed, were like in Andalusia. In the mosques as in that of Sidi bu Medyan near Tlemcen, it was apparently preferred to use piers covered with stucco decoration and join them by horseshoe arches; in the Alhambra the horseshoe arch was avoided, except for the *mihrab*, as we know from the two small oratoria in the palace which are still standing. In the *madrasah* of Fez and Marrakesh wood panelling was used on the walls to a great extent as well as stucco decoration, but even the motifs of the carving remain entirely in the Granadan style. In Rabat this style appears translated into stone on the mausoleum of Abu'l Hassan, while the Shella gate there derives in archaic manner from the Almohad portals of the region. It is interesting here how the decoration spreads on to the two flanking towers, and it appears in even rougher guise on the later palace gate in Meknes.

Even on late monuments like the late 16th century Sa'adite mausoleum the luxuriance of forms is always kept within bounds; strict observance of a discipline dictated by both aesthetic and technical considerations has kept the art of stucco work in Morocco alive to this day. In Tunis and Tripoli it even inspired a resurrection of the Andalusian tradition after it had been forgotten. In the same way faience mosaic, used among other purposes to enliven the minarets with colour and sometimes to decorate public fountains, has remained in general use to the present day in some Moroccan towns for decorating dadoes.

The Mudejar Style

Mudejars are the Muslims who remained true to their faith and customs under Christian rule; they preserved their art and technical skills under the changed circumstances, while seeking to adapt them to the tasks allotted to them by their Christian employers. Since the Spanish centres fell to the reconquest at very different times—Toledo in 1085, Seville in 1248, Granada in 1492—the Mudejar style comprises less a limited period than a movement which set in, now here, now there, but which maintained some continuity of development. The Toledan phase is best illustrated by the two synagogues preserved there: the earlier, of c. 1200, is a pillared hall with blind arcading entirely in the style of Almohad mosques, with very impressive pine-cone capitals (plate 55), the later, c. 1365, is an undivided elongated room with a women's gallery and a facing of stucco in which an attempt is made to marry Moorish architectural motifs and arabesques with Gothic vine scrolls and friezes of Hebraic script. Several Toledan church towers derive closely from the minaret, and in the interior of Christian churches too there are frequently sacristies or single chapels decorated by Muslim stucco workers. Saragossa also showed relatively early a strong Mudejar influx, the cathedral being one example.

After the conquest of Cordova the mosque was converted into a cathedral and a mudejar choir was built into it. A new main portal shows the Alhambra style breaking through; it was soon to dominate the decoration of the Alcazar in Seville. It is true that in the Maidens' Court the motif of the scalloped arch with lozenge trellis above it (plate 58) is probably still to be seen as a translation of the decoration of the Giralda into monumental terms, but its execution in unconnected masses of stucco is already unmistakably Granadine technique, and in the Dolls' Court there is hardly a detail to cast doubt on the provenance of its ornament. Two interesting features in this building are the Arabic epigraphy, with its praises of the king 'Don Pedro', and the careful inclusion of 'Frankish' elements even in the restorations of the 16th century, when we are already in the presence of an almost baroque mudejar. The famous 'Casa de Pilatos' and other palaces in Seville succeeded in combining this tradition with Renaissance ideas. After the 15th century faience mosaic (*alicatado*) was abandoned in favour of square tiles (*azulejos*), and Seville held the lead in their production. They used the techniques of *cuerda seca* and *cuenca* to prevent colours from running together; in the former the outlines are neutralized by running waxed cord round them, the latter is raised relief.

Outside the three centres mentioned the mudejar style appears in many places; panelled ceilings either carved or stepped into honeycomb cells (*artesonados*) were handed over to the traditional skill of Moorish craftsmen who as such found plenty of employment until they became completely absorbed, or else were forcibly driven out (1610).

Moorish Minor Arts

As soon as the period of the archaic Kufic was over, and it ended essentially with the Umayyad period, a characteristic hand prevailed over the whole of western Islam; it is still practised to-day from Morocco to Tripoli and is rightly called the *Mahgrebi*. It is distinguished from the more swelling *Naskhi* by a more vertical stance and a gentler, less emphatic execution which makes it easy to recognize Western manuscripts without further investigation. Title pages, chapter heads, embellishments and border medallions are filled in with interlacing and arabesques in Moorish style, mostly in blue and gold; Valencia will have played a leading role in the 12th-13th centuries; later Korans were illuminated in Granada and Fez entirely in the Alhambra style with rich colour effects (plate 59a).

On the other hand miniatures seem only occasionally to have been included even in secular texts; the explanation may be that the whole development took place during the puritanical epoch of Berber dominance which nipped in the bud any leanings towards painting. Even the remains of wall and ceiling paintings in the Alhambra are no argument against this, for everything points to their having been executed by foreign artists. It is remarkable that the *Mahgrebi* script did not spread to the inscriptions on monuments and utensils whose epigraphic decoration had spent itself, as also happened in the East, in exploiting the decorative possibilities of Kufic and Naskhi.

The art of binding shows the same interlacery and band work in blind tooling as was done in Cairo in the Mamluk period. Ivory carving, which was so important in the Umayyad period and produced such outstanding pieces, faded into insignificance, and it cannot be supposed that boxes and caskets of precious metal could provide a substitute for it. Inlay technique does not seem to have become naturalized in Spain, and even the production of bronze pieces simply engraved or plated with gold leaf is minimal. On the other hand a mosque flask dated 1305 from the Alhambra is evidence of the extraordinary skill of Granadan craftsmen in filigree-like *ajourée* metalwork; its spread out script and scroll ornament seems far superior to contemporary Mamluk work.

Sculptural bronze casting was also attempted; it is known from two identically modelled ewers decorated with engraving which are not far removed in spirit from the lions of the Alhambra fountain. Few ornaments of gold, understandably, have come down to our time; filigree work is considered to be an old Andalusian tradition and examples were made in Granada in the 14th and 15th centuries. Moorish Spain was more important in the sphere of arms and armour. Toledan blades equalled the Damascene in fame; a collection of straight swords from the heyday of Granada has survived, with the hilts and guards executed in punched, pierced and enamelled gold. They all have the same characteristic form with the dragon motif on downward curving quillons and a decorated pommel; they are generally accorded legendary association with the person of Boabdil, the last of the Nasrids. There are also examples in European collections of the so-called 'ear daggers' which are typical of the Moorish region.

The development of faience mosaic and tile production was relatively limited as compared with Persia, the much simpler technical methods, confined to geometric line drawing, made it impossible to emulate the wealth of colour and design of Mongol period Persian work, but in the sphere of ceramic vessels Spain could unashamedly sustain comparison with the luxury wares of the Orient. The speciality of Seville was the production of large water and provision jars with a rich relief ornament, part deeply carved, part moulded, and of fountain heads of similar technique. Malaga was famous throughout the world for her lustre ware, which reached its finest flowering in the 14th century, just at the time when those of Rayy, Kashan and Cairo were declining. In the massive wing-handled vases designed for the state rooms of the Alhambra it introduced a new and individual type of vessel into the ceramic repertoire of Islam (plate 59b). The decoration covers the whole body in different zones of lustre painting, the design either close or loose, on a bare ground or over a close pattern of curls. As in Persia blue was used over the glaze as well as the metal colour; the patterns kept to the repertoire of Alhambra ornament, with a strong leaning towards the arabesque, which spread even to the animal motifs that were used occasionally.

Craftsmen from Malaga carried the technique to Valencia, where it was further developed during the 15th century in the potters' village of Manises, though here, of course, due to the political circumstances, already in a mudejar context. Mangled Arabic script and misunderstood arabesques characterize the first phase, which was soon followed by large animals with Gothic mottoes, vine leaf patterns and flowering sprays with the emblems of Spanish and Italian patrons. Complete services of table ware of the most varied kind were ordered from the workshops, and in Venice and Bruges the costly Valencia wares were a valuable item of import; they were no less so in Alexandria.

Finds of sherds from Old Cairo show how intensive was the import into Egypt, where no offence was taken even at plates and dishes with the device AVE MARIA GRATIA PLENA. The blue colour was used here as well, lavishly or frugally beside the lustre, but this gradually lost its splendid gold colour and in the 16th century was applied to the whole surface in very close patterns, degenerating at last into a soulless coppery daub. Paterna, another pottery near Valencia, produced a plainer ware in the 14th and 15th centuries, with stylized animal figures of striking effect and other motifs, some Gothic, in green and manganese brown painting on a white ground. This also influenced Italian majolica, like the Manises types.

In the production of silk cloth the Andalusian workshops kept step with those of the Orient all through the Middle Ages. The repeat patterns with confronted animals in circles of inscription as known in Baghdad, Palermo and Cairo were also favoured here for a time, and there is evidence that Baghdad silks were faked in Andalusia in the 11th century. Production of gold brocades was on a larger scale, however, with non-animate themes such as a close star pattern with Naskhi borders; examples were found among the burial vestments at Las Huelgas near Burgos and among those of the Infante Don Felipe, of which fragments are preserved in several collections. In the 14th century the Alhambra ceramic style with its many polygonal ribbon inter-laceries seems to have penetrated the workshops of Almeria, which produced mainly for the court of Granada, and similar silk patterns continued for a long time in Fez and other Moroccan workshops. In the 15th century, probably at Valencia and Seville, the *mudejar* style was introduced into the textile sphere in very individual motifs, with unconnected continuous rows of leaf and lotus figures with rampant lions and other such motifs. Old embroideries have been preserved, such as some Merinid war flags of the 14th century in the Cathedral of Toledo; a tent curtain in multi-coloured, very painstaking stitching in Las Huelgas near Burgos is the Almohad booty from the battle of Las Navas (1212).

We have fragments of Spanish knotting of the 12th century; from the texture and coloration we can deduce that the technique immediately developed there along its own lines. It flourished mainly in Alcaraz from the 14th century. Script borders seem to have been in favour here also, and reminiscences of it can be traced in the otherwise entirely mudejar style pieces of the 15th century, in which Spanish emblems among manifold geometric motifs appear on a predominantly blue field. Repetitions of large star-shaped polygons in bright colours dominate the decoration of contemporary Moroccan work to the exclusion of all else; it uses the same plain knot as the Spanish. No examples remain from other regions of the Mahgreb.

ISLAMIC ART
IN
THE MODERN PERIOD

CHAPTER EIGHT

Safavid Art in Persia

IN 1502 a Shi'ite dynasty came to power in Persia with Shah
Isma'il. It honoured the holy Sheikh Safi of Ardebil as its
founder and took its name from him. An unsuccessful war
against the Ottomans drove it back inside Iran's natural frontiers,
and it then turned to realizing the national ideals of the people and
bringing about the last great period of culture. Mongol traditions
were in part rejected, in part exploited in the new spirit, and soon
there were many towns engaged in artistic activity. Tebriz as the
new seat of government began by taking the lead but was later
superseded by Kazvin and in the late 16th century by Isfahan. This
city developed under the assiduous and magnificent reign of Shah
Abbas the Great into one of the most brilliant towns of the Orient,
and in the 17th century it became once more a focus for all the
artistic energy in the country. Characteristic of the period are the
closer ties with China on the one hand, and on the other with
Europe, for the Shah had acumen enough to make important
alliances among the royal courts. In Iraq, which remained united
with Persia until 1638 the Shi'ite pilgrimage centres prospered and
gave the country a last sunset glow of splendour.

Even before the overthrow of the Safavid dynasty in 1722 there
was decadence in every sphere of art. Royal interest slackened,
mass production of cheap bazaar wares became a fixed policy, and
the awakening of Western interest in the Orient showed itself
principally in ignorant admiration and greedy acquisition of
exotic small wares. This all contributed to the general collapse
into stagnation which was soon to come, and which even the

efforts of Fath Ali Shah failed to remedy when he tried to raise the standard of craft work in the early 19th century.

Sacred Building

The tombs that had once been so important for architectural development were still capable of eliciting occasional new forms, although now only in the shape of saints' tombs (*imamzade*). In western Persia these were enlarged into elongated domed buildings by the addition of an annexe, while to the east the pavilion type spread, mostly octagonal with flat *iwan* niches, finding its worldly counterpart in the garden houses with open central hall (see below).

A tomb mosque in the grand manner was started for Sheikh Safi in Ardebil in the 16th century as the extension of an older tomb. It was completed in the middle of the 17th century. A broad square with a ceremonial outer gate is followed by an elongated garden court, to which the groups of buildings are joined at an angle (fig 19). The inner courtyard, 31 by 16 metres in area, has on its left the older very individual mosque. It is an octagon standing on 16 wooden pillars with window recesses and without a *mihrab* (the *qibla* is at the entrance); at a right angle to this mosque lies the mausoleum itself, consisting of a small tomb chamber and a prayer hall with rectangular niches in two storeys. The rather palace-like façade is of great beauty. It is of brick with a tall portal with pointed arch on the left flank, a stalactite frieze marking the horizontal plane and symmetrical rows of windows for vertical articulation. These windows are pierced in patterns and are framed with rich faience mosaic. The centralized building alongside the mausoleum—with a dome on a low drum—is the 17th century Porcelain House (*Chini Khane*) in which the Chinese ceremonial wares of the sanctuary were preserved. The walls had wood panelling with openings of various forms and sizes in which the pieces were individually displayed in close rows reaching as high as the summit of the niche arches. Large kitchens and living rooms for priests, pilgrims and the poor also form part of the complex.

Of the true mosques of this period the Masjid-i-Shah in Isfahan

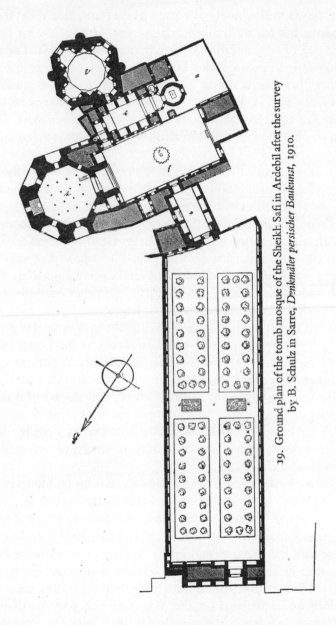

19. Ground plan of the tomb mosque of the Sheikh Safi in Ardebil after the survey by B. Schulz in Sarre, *Denkmäler persischer Baukunst*, 1910.

(plate 60) is undoubtedly the most important, not only for its splendour but for its architectural interest, although even here a slackening of concentration is already making itself felt. The connecting galleries provide the whole with only a loose coherence, and the three *iwan* seem almost like three separate domed buildings. The Gyök Jami' (Yellow Mosque) in Erivan is notable as a domed mosque of the 18th century. It consists of two *iwan* with dome chambers behind them on the narrow sides of an arcaded courtyard.

Isfahan possesses the last great *madrasah* built in Persia, the Shah Sultan Husein (also called Mader-i-Shah, c. 1700). The four *iwan* are arranged round the rectangular court with two storeys of cells and extended on the *qibla* side to a large dome chamber. From the four corners of the court passages lead into smaller courts which also have several storeys of cells. The whole plan is exceptionally monumental and harmonious in its proportions. The Vekil *madrasah* in Shiraz (18th century) and other examples offer little that is new in architecture. More important for the followers of the Shi'a than the buildings on national territory at this period was the erection of splendid tomb mosques at the burial places of their holy *imam* in Mesopotamia. In Kerbala, Nejef, Samarra and other pilgrimage centres sanctuaries were built entirely in Safavid style right into the 19th century, and the faithful make pilgrimages there even to this day; that of Qazimein near Baghdad is supposed to have been completed in 1519 by Shah Isma'il; it has a very clear and compact structure, with gilded domes.

Faience mosaic was still used on most religious buildings in the Safavid period. In Ardebil it is technically in the highest tradition, and even in the Isfahan *madrasah* mentioned above it is still quite outstanding. It is used both inside and outside, on the vaulting of the *iwan*, on the minarets and in the *mihrab* dome, with the most meticulous technique, in effective colours and wonderfully rich designs of flowers and plant scrolls. Even stronger is the impression of colour and ornament on the Masjid-i-Shah with its massive court frontages (plate 60), positively dazzling, with blue dominant in the interior vaulting.

Towns, Palaces and Functional Buildings

The layout of Isfahan as a modern capital is entirely inspired by Shah Abbas the Great; it deserves careful examination as a far-sighted and conscious attempt at town planning. The imposing Royal Square (Meidan-i-Shah) is sited near the centre of the town; it is surrounded by a continuous row of two-storeyed arcades, broken by four tall gatehouses: the Bazaar gate, the 'Ali Qapu leading to the palace, the Lufallah Mosque and the entrance to the Masjid-i-Shah. The axis of the latter deviates from the square because of the *qibla*, but the portal *iwan* is very skilfully placed at a tangent to it, so as to readjust the Meidan frontage. Southwards from the palace are laid out stretches of park with gracious pavilions.

From one of these, the Chihil Sutun, a vista was laid out through the town and over the river to the park of Hezar Jerib, thus creating a promenade of 3 kilometres (the Chehar Bagh) with dwelling palaces, kiosks and fountains, dotted with plane trees, crossed by a canal and bounded at each end with pavilions. Streets were laid parallel to it, and monumental bridges spanned the river. The bridges are boldly conceived with two tiers of arches and terminal and central buildings; they are really only comprehensible in the context of their important function in the layout of the whole town (plate 61). The successors of the great ruler did much building in continuation of his plans, and even the silhouette of the town, as seen from the specific vantage points, is highly successful as a unified panorama and most harmonious in effect. Chardin visited Isfahan at its most brilliant period and he has left us an enthusiastic description of its splendours, sufficiently detailed to allow us to fill in with our imagination what is now lacking.

An innovation in palace design itself was its much greater integration with the surrounding park architecture; hence, logically, the palace assumed a more pavilion-like character. Generally the main room consisted of the highest possible hall, round which dwelling rooms were arranged in two storeys, and sometimes a third was added as an open hall with divided staircase. The first idea of this development must have been inspired by the airy wooden buildings of West Turkestan, some of which were much earlier than this period.

In the Chihil Sutun (Forty Pillars), the throne room built by Shah Abbas I, later destroyed by fire and rebuilt in the 18th century, an open hall is flanked by two closed rooms and deepened by a hall with three domes lying perpendicular to it, for private audiences. This palace lay within a large park, and that of Hesht Bihesht (1670) by even closer association with broad park landscapes realized its architectural aim as a centre for splendid festivities; the dwelling rooms were situated in towers at the four corners. The Mirror Kiosk ('Aine Khane) was laid out like the Chihil Sutun, but was simpler, with one hall with wooden pillars and latticed windows. Other pavilions have perished, understandably, as they were built of flimsy materials; they often also had fountains and other water-works. In the palace-like 'Ali Qapu on the Meidan the kiosk-like character is even carried over to the gateway. The park round Shah Abbas's palace in Ashraf (Mazenderan) was very extensive, it was laid out with water basins and symmetrically placed buildings in strictly Iranian tradition.

Public buildings occupied a more important place in the architecture of this late period than heretofore, and they were often on a grand scale. In the caravanserai the same basic scheme was used as in the *madrasah*, with sleeping cells, stalls and store rooms laid round a courtyard with a ground plan that was always symmetrical, occasionally hexagonal. Sometimes, for example in the building of Sultan Husein in Isfahan, the *madrasah* and the *khan* are closely combined into a single unit. In Mesopotamia the rest houses were built entirely in the Safavid style until a much later time, often with imposing *iwan* arranged round a spacious court. The bazaars in some towns (Isfahan, Shiraz, Kashan) are striking for their monumental effect. They often include baths. Fountains, water tanks and store houses for ice were also sometimes architecturally significant.

As regards interior decoration, tiles took the place of faience mosaic in the Isfahan palaces. In the time of Shah Abbas I tile production was in close contact with the schools of painting of Isfahan. Large-scale compositions were made in square tiles, mostly genre subjects and battle scenes, in strikingly varied and harmoniously combined colours. The different colours were separated by waxed cord, and the methods of glazing made possible great delicacy in the drawing. Parts of such wall facings have often reached public collections, among them some from the palace of Chihil Sutun; in the 18th century the designs become plainer and the colours harsher. About 1600 smaller rectangular tiles with separate motifs in relief and with soft glazes also came into favour and were even let singly into the wall.

Otherwise wood decoration was prevalent in secular building, in keeping with the light pavilion architecture, and here lacquer painting was much used as well as gilding. The motifs again stood in very close relationship to miniature painting. Carving and intarsia were also practised particularly on doors and ceilings. In other cases decorative frescoes were preferred, as for example in 'Ali Qapu and in Ashraf, mostly figure representations in soft tones. An innovation of some grandeur was the use of mirrors in palace rooms; from them the 'Aine Khane received its name. Dadoes were often faced with marble, and the taste for fountains and such like led naturally to a revivification of decorative sculpture.

Adequate facilities for the display of art objects became increasingly more of a necessity with the growth of an interest in collecting, and it became usual to cover walls with wood scaffolding as in the Porcelain Chamber in Ardebil, cut into niches of different shapes to hold single vases. The panelling in the 'Ali Qapu is a characteristic example.

Book Production and Painting

The Safavid period saw the full flowering of what had been begun in the Timurid period, particularly in the Herat school, and it gave to the whole craft a strongly national bias.

The new capital of Tebriz became a centre of production for sumptuous Koran manuscripts, for it harboured the most famous masters in Naskhi and Thuluth and the most prominent illuminators and gilders for ornamenting the text. The composition of the title pages into fields with star or medallion compartments and frames with cartouches and similar ornament was their invention, and their skill in illumination was a considerable influence on other arts, particularly rug making. The type of Koran evolved here remained standard for the following period, not only in Persia, but in Turkey and in India, whither calligraphers and illuminators were summoned from Tebriz during the 16th century. Even more considerable perhaps was the increase in production of secular texts. Innumerable copes of the *shah-nama*, the works of Nizami, of Jami and other Persian poets circulated, and from the close co-operation of calligraphers and painters came superbly beautiful and coherent works of art. Samples of the writing of famous masters of *nast'aliq* like Sultan 'Ali of Meshhed or Mir Ali el-Katib soon became much treasured and after the 16th century were carefully collected (plate 63b).

For both religious and profane manuscripts the bookbinders were also in high demand. In gold tooling they even surpassed the extraordinary achievements of the Mongol period; they enlivened the surface with matrices in various depths of relief, decorating the inner sides with most skilfully manipulated paper filigree; lacquer was now also introduced to decorate the book cover.

The liberation of the Herat miniature school from the conventional Mongol style and the founding of a national style of painting based on a healthy realism was the work of the great Behzad. His work, though begun in the last third of the 15th century, was fully in the style which became general after the Safavid revolution. He removed to the court of Tebriz in 1506 and was active there until after 1520. Unlike his precursors he no longer had texts supplied from the calligraphers but himself chose the material to be treated and preferred whole page or even two-page compositions (plate 62). His main concern was for untrammelled postures and facial differentiation of the figures, and he used to this end an exceptionally rich palette, particularly in the dark tones. The number of authentic works from his hand is small. His fame spread rapidly beyond the frontiers of Persia, and ever since the 16th century pages which wrongly bear his name, either copies or fakes, have abounded.

Behzad had many gifted pupils who worked in the spirit of his reforms in the many studios where book illustration was practised.

They created new schemes for the illumination of luxury copies of the great Persian poets and these became standard for future generations. One of Behzad's pupils, Mahmud Mudhahib, created the special style of the school of Bokhara; another, the outstandingly gifted Sultan Muhammad, attained great influence about the middle of the 16th century as Director of the Academy and Gallery under Shah Tahmasp, encouraging particularly the fashion of the collector's album (*muraqqa*), in which examples of calligraphy and sketches or miniatures by famous masters could be assembled. This changed the type of work commissioned from painters: instead of the handling of epic themes the demand was for portraiture and genre studies for special occasions.

The observation of nature and the representation of everyday reality which had been thus stimulated was raised to an artistic principle in the school of Isfahan, where Riza 'Abbasi (plate 63a) stood out as the most remarkable personality, followed by a large host of imitators who continued to work in his style until the 18th century. Although he is Persian in every stroke of his brush, in the choice of his motifs and in the surety of their rendering in rapid brush sketches he stands unmistakably close to the Dutch masters of the 17th century. This reflects a general tendency, for the contact with European art in which the great Shah showed so much interest could not fail to influence developments in Persia. Besides many imitations we possess a large number of genuine pages with the signature of Riza, and notes in his own hand about the subject; often these are fleeting sketches, jotted down with great mastery and sure observation of nature.

Textiles and Carpets

The painting style of the 16th and 17th centuries penetrated into almost every sphere of craft and enlivened greatly the motifs of the textile crafts, which at that time reached the most brilliant achievements of which they have ever been capable. Alexander's fight with the dragon or Leila's visit to Majnun in summarily crisp figures, or genre types of lovers, revellers and single figures are repeated in rows over the length of the cloth, either in separate compartments or with skilful transitions through tree, spray or plant scroll pattern (plate 64a). We find simultaneously multi-coloured light silks, heavy gold and silver brocades and sheared velvets. The latter in particular have no equal in the tenderness of the drawing and harmonious combination of the colours, which change at each repeat. Very few whole garments have survived from this period; usually the costly stuffs sent by Shah Abbas I as presents to Europe survive as fragments of varying sizes in public and private collections, and only exceptionally do we meet them even as wall hangings (in the Rosenborg castle in Copenhagen). It is to be presumed that they were thus used in the Isfahan palaces, at least those with the large figured patterns. Even richer than the figurative repertoire was that of ornamental motifs, among which plant representations in bunches or garlands were predominant.

Information on the places of production is uncertain. Isfahan played an essential role and seems to have made particular classes of wares at the court factory; Kashan is also named, and Yezd in southern Persia was still leading the velvet industry in the 18th century. In the Safavid period silk embroidery took on a new lease of life, mainly in the north-west and in the Caucasus region, with colourful dress coats and coverlets which left a long tradition in folk art.

The 16th century is the classic period of the Persian rug industry. In the state workshops under the direction of highly gifted artists it achieved a perfection of graphic delicacy, wealth of colour and manual dexterity such as this craft had never known. There are basically two categories: the more numerous with a strongly centralized pattern, the other with a pattern in one direction up the length. In the latter category belong the so-called vase rugs, with large and varied flower motifs connected by thin leaf scrolls and interrupted now and then by wing-handled vases out of which the whole maze of flowers must originally have grown symmetrically (plate 64b). The usual narrow border invites the suggestion that these rugs were primarily designed to lie side by side, several together, stressing the *qibla* orientation in mosque sanctuaries—a designation which is supported by the absence of animate subjects in the decoration.

They show connections with pieces produced in the previous Mongol period in the Caucasus. These argue for their own provenance in north-west Persia, but lately this once accepted theory has been discredited in favour of a more southern origin in Kirman. The so-called garden rugs with their harder drawing are, however, certainly from the north; their design patently imitates the Persian park with its central basin, lateral canals, tree-lined avenues and flower beds. This scheme continued virtually unaltered into the 18th century. One-way repeat patterns are also seen in rugs with alternate trees with leaves and blossom, either separate or in groups, which probably came from southern Persia.

The rugs with central design, divided into four symmetrical fields, were originally intended to lie singly on the floor of a room, either large or small; the framing border was naturally wider and heavier on these, and deliberately contrasted with the field in colour and design. The centre was generally emphasized by a round or oval central medallion on a contrasting ground, and it was often given smaller additions above and below; when corner sections were added in the corresponding colour the connection with book illustration becomes particularly plain. When these medallion rugs were intended for religious purposes they also had the field closely covered with flower scrolls, but drawn smaller and in a more fluid manner than on the vase rugs; an exceptionally sumptuous example from the mosque in Ardebil, dated 1539 (now in the Victoria and Albert Museum, London), has large lamps hanging into the field from the central star with its ogival surround. The border was usually filled with palmette flowers between cloud banks or arabesques; another favourite was an alternation of elongated cartouches and rosettes, which seem entirely derived from book bindings.

In the secular luxury pieces of this type the ground was often scattered with trees among which appeared a tumult of animals, some naturalistic, some taken from the Chinese world of fable, without any relation to each other beyond a strictly symmetrical arrangement (plate 65). In these cases the central medallion was often filled with flying birds, and in the borders the palmettes sometimes turned into animal masks, and the arabesques into pheasants; in the cartouches again there sometimes appeared Persian verses in Taliq hand. Animal decoration came into its own in the large hunting rugs, in which whole scenes were depicted with huntsmen on horseback. The most famous of such pieces came to the Österreichisches Museum in Vienna from the Habsburg court collection; it is in knotted silk, brocaded with gold and silver threads and was certainly designed by Sultan Muhammad or some other outstanding painter of the period, with an incomparably beautiful border in which angels form the main motif against a background of soft flower scrolls with small birds. An equally important hunting rug, but of wool, with the date 1542 and probably from the factory in Tebriz, is in the Museo Poldi Pezzoli in Milan.

The first stage in the evolution of the hunting rug seems to have followed on a reduction or suppression of the central medallion, so that the composition could be drawn freely over the whole field, though some feeling for centralization still remained; but in other cases the device was adopted of enclosing animals, horsemen, plant motifs etc in individual cartouches and covering the surface with definite rows of these. In the late 16th century a new type arose as well, probably in Herat. These are mainly nonfigurative rugs, with a claret field covered principally by palmette flowers and cloud bands, but in contrast to the vase rugs the design was conceived outwards from the centre. The border was always green or blue. These 'Herat' rugs seem to have enjoyed particular success in Portugal, where originals are still preserved in strikingly large quantities. The term 'Portuguese rugs', however, is used, not for these but for south Persian products on which the corner sections have representations of boats with Europeans in them.

The so-called Polish rugs form a special category of the period of Shah Abbas. They bear this deceptive name because the Polish eagle was identified on a few of them and their provenance thus mistakenly deduced. Meanwhile similar pieces have been found in nearly every European court, and in many cases it has been possible to prove that they were brought by Persian diplomats of the period. It is now established that the uncharacteristic but now naturalized class of design is a product of the Persian court factory, made principally for gifts to the West. The rugs are always made of silk, with interruptions in the knotting which were then filled in with brocading in gold or silver thread. They can be distinguished from other groups immediately on account of the lighter palette (plate 66). They use the most varied patterns for the designs. Woven tapestry rugs were also used for the same purpose (*kelims*) again of silk and in numerous different patterns.

We are not yet clear as to the exact provenance of the various types enumerated above, and the theories advanced are none of them reliably documented. In the 18th century production fell everywhere into a decadent phase; the patterns disintegrate and are jumbled together, and nothing remains of the earlier golden age but a manual dexterity which even today can produce a fine floor covering, but is not entirely satisfying as a design or colour scheme.

Weapons and Ceramics

Domestic utensils of metal were rather insignificant in this period; tinned copper vessels were much in favour. In the armourer's craft, however, the new period brought many changes from Mongol practices. In place of the straight Mongol sword came the curved sabre, and the elegant Safavid blades carried the fame of the swordsmiths of Isfahan far beyond the frontiers of the land. Besides rich gold inlay of ornaments and inscriptions they are sometimes decorated as well with pictures in artistic engraving in the steel, and this also spread on to quillons and parts of the belt. Daggers (*khanjar*) with a slightly curved edge were common at this time, and about 1500 the type of dagger was evolved in Herat which was to become the model for centuries to come. Battle axes of carved steel or iron have also a characteristic form in this period, and very fine examples of Persian helmets, which have survived in quite large numbers, show decorative techniques such as relief carving and gold inlay at the height of their powers. In shape too they are entirely different from those of the Mongol period, and they are smaller in size, since they did not have to fit over a turban, but were worn directly on the head. We know also a few examples of round parade shields with protruding boss, and some pieces of armour show the technique of inlay still in its heyday in the 17th century.

Attempts had been made in the Middle Ages to produce a transparent and unscratchable porcellanous ware from ordinary faience, and these were resumed in the Safavid period with much zeal, so as to counter with home produce the enormously increased import trade from China. The blue porcelains made for the Islamic Orient were especially successfully imitated in dishes, ewers, plates and bowls. They not only kept as closely as possible to the typical Far Eastern decoration but came so close to their models in technique that for some time it was even dared to offer them to the European market as true porcelain. Thus they achieved their aim completely; under Shah Abbas production seems to have been very extensive, and it continued into the 18th century.

The name of that great ruler is especially associated with another ware, a hard semi-porcelain which for the last time brought honour to lustre work; it too derived from the Ming style; for a short time really magnificent wares were produced: bottles, bowls and cups which vie with the products of the Middle Ages in the purity of their gold colour.

Thin, mostly coloured, blown glass bottles for sprinkling rose water, and decorative ewers and vases show that the Safavids also succeeded in breathing new life into the glass industry of their country, for a time. Examples of this craft are to be seen in most museums of arts and crafts.

CHAPTER NINE

The Mughal Style in India

THERE was no smooth transition from mediaeval Delhi to the epoch which decided the fate of Islamic India from the 16th century onwards. As had already happened under the Ghaznevids and the Ghorids, a new conquest from Afghanistan introduced the change. This time it was a descendant of Timur who first occupied Kabul from west Turkestan and then by various stages created for himself a kingdom in Hindustan which was to last two hundred years.

The Timurid dynasty which came to rule in India with Babur and is known as that of the Great Mughals developed what was already recognizable in the preceding Pathan period into a rich Indo-Islamic style. For long, art historians did not recognize the independence of this style and regarded it as an offshoot of Persian art, being misled by the evident contrast to the pure Hindu stream. Only gradually has it been seen that though these monuments are often superficially reminiscent of Iranian forms, they are primarily the creation of indigenous traditions, and in any case follow an entirely original development. Persian influence is most noticeable under Humayun (1530–1556), who was driven into exile for many years by rebellions and lived then at the court of Shah Tahmasp; but under Akbar (1556–1605) it paled completely in face of the renaissance of Indian national ideals which this enlightened and far-seeing ruler encouraged in every sphere. They bore their richest fruit under his successors Jehangir and Shah Jehan (1628–1659). In the 18th century this movement gave way to a pleasant but infertile eclecticism, which then slowly dwindled into stagnation.

The capital at first was Agra, then from 1569-1583 Fatihpur Sikri, a magnificent new city founded by Akbar, later Lahore, then Agra again and lastly Delhi, which re-emerged in the 17th century. Unfortunately the remains of this epoch, like those of the earlier ones, now all lie in ruins.

Apart from the Mughal emperors several Muslim princes were outstanding as builders; in the crafts the cultural expansion of the 16th and 17th centuries was mainly confined to textiles and minia-ture painting, which here achieved an importance unrivalled in other Islamic countries.

Funerary Buildings and Mosques

The most important of late Islamic buildings in India are un-doubtedly the mausolea, which assumed unusually monumental forms and are of prime significance for a conspectus of the archi-tecture of the time. Although the problem of the dome was being solved in a characteristic Indian form before the end of the pre-ceding period (see p. 96), it was not until now that the ultimate lotus or onion shape reached its distinctive formulation. One of its main uses was of course on the royal tombs, which combined most felicitously with Indian garden architecture in the novel shape of four- or eight-sided pillared pavilions with verandahs of pointed arches. They were sited carefully in the middle of a pond or as the focus of a delightfully laid out park, and the weight of the structure was lightened by deep alcoves or open galleries, or by decorative supporting kiosks.

The most interesting 16th century example is the tomb of the Sher Shah in Sahsaram, which rises as a compact mass of terraces out of the water; that of the Emperor Akbar in the park of Sik-andra is a long hall with airy multi-storeyed galleries, evidently derived from the Vihara type of Indian monastery. The most ambitious of these mausolea and perhaps the most beautiful of all time is the famous Taj Mahal at Agra (plate 67b), built between 1630 and 1648 by Shah Jehan in memory of his wife after her early death. It is picturesquely sited at the end of a rectangular garden crossed by water basins, with the river Jumna behind. It is entirely faced with glistening marble, against which the neighbouring buildings of red sandstone make an effective contrast. Persian influences can be seen in the articulation of the façade, but in all other details, the rounding of the corners, the contour of the dome, the form of the four flanking corner towers, and in the finish of the interior the Indian note sets the key. The design is a clearly thought out and harmonious whole, so much so that it was long before people would relinquish the idea that a European architect must have been in charge.

The tomb of 'Itimad ed-daula (1610) can be regarded as a forerunner of the Taj: the four corner towers were still attached to the pavilion. A contrast is the mausoleum of Mahmud 'Adil Shah in Mijapur (c. 1660) which is conceived entirely in terms of weight and mass, and returns to this form, fitting the towers now directly into the square of the walls. They are given seven storeys of pierced windows to balance the weight of the mighty dome (38 metres in diameter).

In mosque building, too, old traditions were carried on in the Mughal period; in large mosques the separation of the different components destroys the unity of the whole, and the monumentality of the buildings is principally to be sought in their size. An important example from the second half of the 16th century is the Chief Mosque of Bijapur, with a large dome chamber in the centre and small domes over each supporting square of the pillared hall. The mosque of Fatihpur Sikri has three prayer chambers side by side on one of the narrow sides of a gigantic arcaded court and a high pavilion-like gatehouse on one of the long sides. The great mosque in Agra, also begun by Akbar, was completed by Jehangir, who also built the one in Lahore, while Delhi did not have one until Shah Jehan. The Delhi mosque spreads out over a huge terrace, and is planned on a large and noble scale, with a three-storeyed gatehouse and a strongly emphasized façade dominated by the tall entrance *iwan* and bound in by two slender minarets; behind it rise the three onion tops of the *haram* (plate 68b). Shah Jehan raised his Pearl Mosque (Moti Masjid) between 1648 and 1655 inside the palace complex at Agra; for perfection of form it is scarcely to be equalled. It is of red sandstone, the inside faced entirely with white marble, using elegantly moulded cusped arches. The same name is given to the smaller palace mosque in Delhi erected in 1659 by Aurangzeb, entirely in marble.

In general the Persian influence is more strongly marked in mosques than in the other buildings of the Mughal period in which Indian atavism and the demands of the landscape were dominant. A characteristic peculiarity is the detached and very monumentally conceived portal built in front of the mosque itself.

Palaces and Castles

The Hindu palaces of the 15th century continued mediaeval traditions at least to some extent, and so formed a link between the Mughal period and the Islamic past of India. Under Akbar the Hindu elements were still somewhat in the foreground, in keeping with his religious tolerance and rather nationalistic outlook. It is only under his successors that Hindu characteristics disappear in favour of an unadulterated Indian-Muhammadan style.

Akbar's most important foundation was the new capital of Fatihpur Sikri. It was surrounded on three sides by a 5 kilometre wall, and on the fourth faced an artificial lake. It was provided with palaces and dwellings for the court and administration, mosques, bazaars etc, but in 1585 the seat of government was moved to Lahore, and Fatihpur Sikri was completely abandoned and never again occupied; it has thus remained relatively well preserved. There seems to have been no thought of town planning in its design, which is very irregular. Each building can really only be judged on its own merits—in isolation from the rest. It includes the great throne room (Diwan-i-'Am), the Panj Mahal, a five-storeyed structure of open halls stepped upwards in the old Indian manner of house building, and above all the Diwan-i-Khas for private audiences, a two-storeyed square pavilion with four doors, and a central pillar which carries the ceiling on stalactite brackets. This ceiling is so cut away that only a circular platform and surrounding bridges and galleries remain (plate 68a). Outside, as in the Taj Mahal, the four corners are roofed with open domes, a feature which was henceforth to remain characteristic of Indian palace architecture. Also worthy of note in Fatihpur Sikri are the decorative single-roomed house of the Rumi Sultana, with a square water basin, and the palace of the Jodh Bay, with one of its stepped upper storeys roofed with keeled barrel vaults, following the dictates of the wood of which it is constructed, and with a Hawa Mahal (wind house) consisting simply of a ring of bay windows—a form which was frequently copied later. The dwelling kiosk which first belonged to the *harim* and was later called after the Raja Birbal shows a classic combination of separate rooms, halls and open platforms over an approximately swastika-shaped ground plan. In the upper storey the rooms only touch at one corner, to create the open platforms.

Another work of Akbar's is the castle in Agra built in 1566 of red sandstone; he repeatedly occupied it, for the last time from 1600 to 1605. The main mass of the wall with the great Delhi Gate is his, and also the Red Palace erroneously attributed to Jehangir. Here Persian ideas are more in evidence, but the individual shapes and methods of construction remain Indian. A highly individual effect is achieved in one of the rooms by stone buttresses, and in another by stepped pillar brackets with carved projections, both unmistakably derived from the local woodworking style. Lastly the same Emperor erected between 1572 and 1575 a palace in the famous mediaeval town of Ajmir, where he often liked to stay. It is a simple court surrounded by single rooms with a gatehouse added on one side and large octagonal towers in the corners, just like the large Persian caravanserai. A small villa stands isolated in the centre (*baradari*).

In the 17th century, palace architecture evolved an exceptionally fine feeling for rhythmic values by abandoning ornamental details and emphasizing the structural forms more strongly. Next to nothing survives from the time of Jehangir; the style blossomed in the time of Shah Jehan, who is probably himself mainly responsible for the almost musical temperament of the architecture of his time. Unfortunately only isolated buildings remain, and since they were all so carefully planned with regard to the effect of the whole complex, and their relation to each other, they cannot do themselves justice when isolated from their original context. In the palace already mentioned in Agra there remains a Diwan-i-'Am for formal receptions. It is an open seven-aisled, pillared hall projecting into the courtyard space, with the scalloped arches which are typical of the whole period. Behind it lies the more intimate Diwan-i-Khas with a garden court. This is a transverse room of marble, finely proportioned, with large doors and a pillared gallery in front. The buildings for the *harim* (Zenana) formed another special unit dominated by the pillared banqueting hall (Khas Mahal), and before which a garden was laid out. There are also several separate pavilions, some of great architectural interest.

In the palace at Delhi the courts with their halls are completely destroyed, but luckily the plans have survived, so that the ruins can give us an adequate picture of the vanished splendour of the court of the Great Mughals. The fort-like character was stressed even here by an outer wall, and the general layout was dictated by the suburb, called Shahjahanabad after the Emperor, which grouped itself in a crescent round the castle, with the river in the background. The palace itself covers a rectangle with the reception rooms (court of honour and throne rooms with sandstone pillars) and the private rooms at the centre. Among the latter the Diwan-i-Khas was not shut off as at Agra, but open on all sides, with a flat roof on rectangular piers and scalloped arches. Here too there were gardens dotted with pavilions.

In Lahore the castle built by Akbar in 1584 lay outside the town. The Shish Mahal (hall of mirrors, see below) is one of the 17th century buildings of residence there. The miniatures of Indian painters can be accepted as wholly reliable in their representations of palaces and gardens which have completely disappeared: some of them show charmingly disposed kiosks and pavilions, others have extensive park architecture with river works and other landscape effects (plate 70).

Architectural Ornament

The splendour-loving period of Akbar was especially given to construction in red sandstone, a tradition persisting from Hindu times. Ornamental sculpture naturally flourished with it. It covered every surface with patterns showing connections with the Safavid and Ottoman repertoire. Later came a leaning towards more sober forms, and the stone was overlaid with a polished plaster suitable for painted decoration. After the 17th century the use of marble facing brought to the fore two techniques in which India became supreme: one was the fine lace-like openwork used on marble window fillings and lattices, seen at its best in the Taj Mahal and the mosque on the citadel of Ahmedabad (northern India); the other is the inlay work in marble with various semi-precious stones. This gives the delightful colour effects of the audience hall in the Delhi palace, with its free designs of single bunches of flowers and delicate plant scrolls. In the Shish Mahal at Lahore 'mirror mosaic' was used on the ceilings and upper walls. Thin fragments of coloured glass are pieced together in the stucco ground in patterns of many kinds, often reminiscent of rugs or book covers. The finer details of the drawing are achieved by utilizing even the lines of stucco squeezed out between the fragments. Below this pieces of glass variously shaped into vases and vessels are set in the arcading to give the illusion of display niches, such as are known at Ardebil; the same mosaic decoration was employed in the Palace of the Rajahs at Amber (plate 69).

Ceramic had never been used to any great extent in India for interior decoration, and was now completely abandoned; neither in faience mosaic nor in tiling are there any monuments to compare even remotely with those of Persia. In the later Mughal period large surfaces were occasionally decorated with figure paintings, which are basically translations of book miniatures on a large scale.

Miniature Painting

Just as the interest of the princes in Persia gave the necessary encouragement to the arts of the book, so in India it was the grace and caprice of the rulers that decided the fortunes of the painters' guild. It was chained to the Imperial court until well after the mid-17th century, and expanded there to an extent hitherto unknown. Certainly the continuous intervention from a higher quarter was not without its disadvantages to the artistic quality of the work; independent talents suffered under the constricting demands of the patron, and we find that over the whole period there is an extremely high average standard, and a large amount of very gifted work, but no single personality of towering genius able to open up new vistas for generations ahead. The period as a whole is characterized, apart from a new painting technique, by a strong realism and an interest in representing depth of space through horizontal perspective: a concern entirely contrary to Islamic practice hitherto.

After the first phase in the 16th century the illumination of manuscripts played a subsidiary role, and the main development took place within the sphere created by the fashion for collectors' albums, that is, in the production of single pages. Even in the few cases where texts were illustrated, the independence of the pictures from the text exemplifies this change. The first move in the foundation of a school of Mughal painting was made by painters drawn to the court of Babur from Bukhara and Kabul. They brought certain variants of the Behzad style to India, but from the beginning they advocated new principles of colour, which became standard henceforth. Under Humayun Persian influence was revived, and it was Akbar who first created the groundwork for a national style by appointing Hindu painters. These had grown up in a completely different tradition, stemming from the Ajanta frescoes. He commissioned illustrations of Indian tales and epics, and giant editions of the popular fantastic adventure romance, Amir Hamza. In these illustrations a highly developed and expressive art is used for the dramatic treatment of traditional subjects.

Jehangir was a passionate collector, and prided himself on being the greatest connoisseur of painting of his age. Some of the most brilliant work of the period was done on ornamental borders in various shades of gold over softly coloured underpaintings, done to frame examples of calligraphy by famous masters. But under Jehangir court scenes, portraits and studies of nature came into fashion; specialists like the animal painters Mansur and Murad (plate 72a) rose to distinction, and the trend towards realism was further encouraged by acquaintance with Western paintings and prints. Their naturalism makes these pictures valuable as cultural documents; the representations of imperial audiences and receptions (*durbar*), religious festivities and hunting expeditions, for example, portray all the participants with great fidelity (plate 71), and there is hardly an important personage of this epoch of whom a lifelike portrait does not survive. Jehangir even had likenesses taken of his parade elephants, favourite horses and hunting falcons, and at every notable event his first thought was to have it recorded in a picture. With all this landscape was not neglected, and even nuances of atmosphere and mood were hinted at in the most delicate manner. This shift to purely realistic representational art completely contradicts all the previous attitudes of Islam, which only considered a composition from a decorative point of view. It can be understood as interpreting the attitude to life of the rulers, each of whom took his time so seriously that he recorded it in memoirs, often with great candour.

The period of Shah Jehan brought few innovations in miniature painting; in portraits what counted was the modelling of the head, and accessories were deliberately excluded. Under the strict and puritanical regime of Aurangzeb (1659–1707) the majority of painters lost their positions at court, and when the art was revived in the 18th century it was in a popularizing style which rejoiced in sentimental and romantic themes (plate 72b) and drew eclectically on earlier models. *Ragini*, which are pictorial interpretations of musical rhythms and modes taken over from Hindu art, were much in favour (plate 73a). Painting now began to flourish at the courts of the Rajput princes, owing part of its inspiration to the Mughal school; we are indebted to them most of all for a charming series of pictures illustrating the legend of Krishna (plate 73b).

Calligraphy and binding were practised alongside book illustration, but they cannot compare with Persian work except perhaps in some fine lacquer covers, with predominantly floral patterns.

Textiles and Carpets

In 17th century Muslim India the production of brocades and velvets received a noteworthy impetus from the influence of the south Persian textile industry; the most characteristic patterns were balanced arrangements of loose flower sprays and stylized single flowers, and these were varied in many ways. They are not always easy to distinguish from Persian work. Embroidery remained on the whole a cultivated folk art; in the 18th century in Kashmir the fashion grew up for closely embroidered woollen cloths. These soon reached as far as Europe where the patterns were transferred to weaving.

Knotted rugs were made in the Mughal empire from the early 16th century. Persian influence is more evident in the examples with purely ornamental designs, often corresponding to weaving patterns than in the animal rugs which had their own style right from the beginning. The designers simply did not feel at home with the dictates of strict symmetry in the arrangement of their motifs, they went on to purely pictorial compositions and so reached complete pictures very close in feeling to book miniatures and particularly to lacquer painting (plate 74). Very beautiful ideas were devised for the border, now reduced simply to a frame. The artistic demands on the craftsmen were of the highest order, since any repetition was eliminated. On the technical side the close and regular knotting enabled them to reach a velvet effect which brings the products of the Indian court factories right to the forefront of the craft in this classic period of the rug industry.

CHAPTER TEN

The Ottoman Style

IN the 14th century in Asia Minor the political picture changes; the power of the Seljuks was transferred to a number of smaller local dynasties, and then to the Turkish tribe named after its founder Othman. He contented himself with the Sultanate of Rum, but set himself the task of destroying the Byzantine Empire and carrying Islam across the Bosporus. This he achieved in 1362 with the capture of Adrianople, while Constantinople itself was not conquered for almost another hundred years (1453), when it became the capital of a new world empire. In the middle of the 16th century it stretched from Hungary and the Adriatic to Mesopotamia and Egypt; the assumption of the Caliphate and the possession of the holy places in Arabia assured it enormous religious authority, and the Turkish admirals carried its flag across every sea. Algeria at this time developed under Turkish suzerainty into a pirate state which was the terror of the European trading fleets. The example of Stambul caused a change in the character of oriental cities: Damascus, Baghdad and Mecca were subject to its influence no less than Cairo, Tunis and Algiers.

It is remarkable that in spite of the enormous concentration of artistic powers in Constantinople and the marked privileges for the European provinces, there was such a tremendous upsurge of craft activity even in the Anatolian mother country; the workshops of Brusa, Nicaea and Kutahia provided cloth and faiences for the whole empire and even for export abroad, and the advances in the rug industry were almost exclusively to the advantage of the workshops of Asia Minor.

But fate also ordained for this region a close contact with the West, which facilitated the entry of foreign influence. In architecture, after a helpless period of stagnation, it led to complete capitulation to modern European building styles, in craftwork to soulless mass production of bazaar goods for the Western market.

Mosque Building in the 14th and 15th Centuries

Continuity with the Seljuk period is clearly recognizable in Ottoman sacred building of the 14th century. In Brusa, which had a short period of prosperity as a centre, the transition to the grand style which set in after the conquest of Constantinople is especially plain. The Ulu Jami' there (late 14th century, plate 75a) represents the typical multi-aisled, regular pillared hall with a small cupola over each crossing; in the central aisle one of these is kept as the remnant of a court, with a water basin. The light falls through windows in the drums of the cupolas. The scheme was used in a number of mosques in Anatolia and also in the earliest in Rumelia. Where buildings on a smaller scale were wanted, they put one larger domed hall with an entrance hall; in other cases the ground plan of the Persian domed mosque was used, like that known from the mosque at Tebriz (cf. fig 16). As a rule two vaulted halls were set together, and rooms placed on either side of them, again with the characteristic entrance hall in front.

This type of mosque is seen first in the Imare in Nicaea, is amalgamated with the madrasah plan in the building of Murad I in Brusa, and reaches its perfection there too in the Yeshil Jami' completed in 1424 by Ilia 'Ali. This has a two-storeyed frontage, a portal still in Seljuk tradition and a fountain court laid out in front. Diez found connections with the Mamluk architecture of Cairo in the madrasah of Murad I just mentioned, and in the mosque of Ayasoluk at Ephesos (1375): the former in its plan, the latter in the articulation of its façade, shows a relation to the tomb mosque of Sultan Hassan in Cairo.

A few smaller mosques erected in Stambul in the 15th century adopted the Brusa scheme with a ground plan influenced by the madrasah; to these belong those named after their founders: the jami' of Mahmud Pasha (1464), Murad Pasha (c. 1470) and 'Atyq

'Ali Pasha (1497). The large mosques were naturally subject to the strong influence of the Aghia Sophia after this had been transformed into a mosque. It inevitably guided the imagination of the Turkish architects to grandiose spatial concepts along the lines of Justinian's church. These were already attempted in the Mehmediya erected by Muhammad the Conqueror between 1463 and 1469. Its traditional ascription to the Greek Christodulos has recently had well-founded doubts cast upon it. Indeed it is scarcely credible that a Christian architect reared in the Byzantine school should have been so able to immerse himself in the spirit and forms of the Turkish tradition that he could be able to work out the possibilities implicit in them in a really ambitious and tradition-forming design, under the influence of the Aghia Sophia. The architect adopted from this model the dome system in a somewhat simplified form which emphasized the cross plan (without galleries, and with four equally large half-domes) and laid out in front of the whole building a fountain court of almost the same dimensions with domed arcades surrounding it. The building is changed in many respects by frequent destructions and restorations, and cannot serve today as a reliable document. The next important mosque, carried out by the architect Kheir ed-din at the order of the Sultan Bayazid between 1501 and 1507, is more enlightening in some details (plate 75b). In ground plan it followed the Aghia Sophia more strictly and, like it, has side aisles each with four small domes; the minarets stand at the ends of the façade of the sanctuary which extends beyond the breadth of the court on either side. They have the spire form with interrupting balconies (sherife), presaged in the squatter Seljuk mosque towers, which is characteristic of Constantinople. The needle shape contrasts effectively with the heavy masses of the vaulting. The Bayazidiye is altogether most felicitously proportioned. It founded a tradition in many details, particularly in the use of the stalactite capital and of colour alternation in the arches.

Sinan and his School

Sinan (d. 1578) was an artist of such outstanding genius that like the leading men of the Renaissance he set the imprint of his personality on a whole epoch. Sixteenth century Turkish architecture saw in his work all the possibilities of its style brought to their most telling and most monumental expression. It has been disputed whether he was Greek or Albanian in origin: but since his work remained Turkish through and through, down to the finest detail, this dispute is irrelevant. The phases of his own development are best illustrated in three buildings, which he himself declared show him as apprentice, journeyman and master.

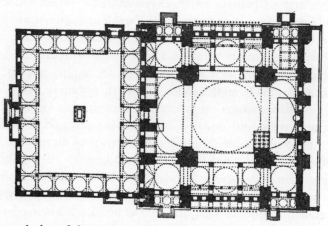

20. Ground plan of the Mosque of the Sultan Sulayman in Istanbul (without surrounding buildings), after C. Gurlitt, *Die Baukunst Konstantinopels*, 1912.

In the Shahzade mosque (1543–1548) he adopts the ground plan of the Mehmediye but attempts to enhance the external lightness of the dome and the harmony of the interior. In the Sulaymaniye (1550–1556, fig 20) he reverts to the Bayazidiye and the Aghia Sophia itself, contenting himself with two half-domes, each on two exedrae, and utilizing again the gallery motif, deliberately centralizing the whole structure; the four corner dome chambers serve as vestibules. He enhances the effect of the façade with a handsome two-tiered gallery in which the lower range has dissimilar arches, and by skilful echeloning of the dome sequence he achieves a unified silhouette which is underlined by the two minarets. Inside he seeks to use the breadth and height of the domed space to mitigate the massive static weight of the structure; the bearing piers at the crossing seem almost slender in the light which streams across the space in every direction, and illuminates the captivating harmony of its proportions (plate 76).

In his masterpiece, the Selimiye in Adrianople, he equals the breadth of span of the dome of Aghia Sophia. He sets the gigantic vaulting on eight twelve-sided piers, lays pillared galleries with tribunes round about, and pierces the walls with innumerable windows so as to banish the last hint of weight and pressure. Four towers make a symmetrical framing for the sanctuary, and here again a fountain court of equal size lies in front of it.

Many other mosques in Constantinople are by Sinan, who according to his own notes erected no less than 318 buildings, and whose personality lived on in the generations that followed him. This is especially the case in the Ahmediye (1608–1614), which in some ways laid the keystone on his endeavour. In the ground plan it follows the Mehmediye and Shahzade mosques, but this time the supports are pillar-like fluted piers, and the two outer corners of the courtyard are given minarets, increasing the number to six. The Yeni Walide Jami', begun in 1651 by Khoja Qasim, takes from the Sulaymaniye the motif of lateral façade with a gallery and eaves, and has a particularly effective dome structure; in the upper storey there are also private rooms for the royal entourage, combined with the galleries. Sinan's style of building did not remain in the Rumelian towns alone but infiltrated into Damascus, Mecca, Cairo and Algiers, and thus brought the challenge of the domed mosque to regions which had until now ignored it, or at any rate had not rightly understood it.

The mosques founded by the Sultans were as a rule surrounded by various tomb chapels (turbe) for their families. They were always domed, but though of manifold design were seldom of architectural significance, and on the whole reflected closely the larger sacred building. Besides this each mosque, according to the extent of its endowment had further annexes: teaching rooms, libraries, baths, and sometimes shops, alms kitchens, hospitals and hostels. The largest of these subsidiary complexes is attached to the Sulaymaniye. The simple forms of the buildings are always comfortably subordinated to the main building.

Secular Building

The Turkish dwelling house (*konak*) was generally built of wood in several storeys; below lay the reception rooms (*selamlik*), above, the family rooms (*harim*); the upper storey projected over the street in the form of a bay window, supported by diagonal struts. Shelved alcoves and a special form of chimney piece with high faceted canopy articulated the surfaces of the walls. The *qa'a* was adopted from Syria and its walls were richly decorated, while a fountain usually played in the centre.

The palaces (*saray*) were similar in detail to the dwelling houses, but the more solid building materials suggested quite other possibilities. Nothing remains of the Ottoman residence in Brusa, and the first palace on European soil, begun by Murad I in 1362 in Adrianople was unfortunately completely destroyed in 1878. It employed the usual division into three, known for instance from the Alhambra. The Old Saray in Stambul, separated from the town by a special dressed stone wall with towers and gates, had originally the same arrangement round three different courts, but later extensive enlargements have blurred it somewhat. The earliest part surviving is the Chinili Köshk (Faience Pavilion) built in 1472 by the Persian architect Kemal ed-din. It is laid out as a cross inside a square, with a projecting polygonal apse, central dome, corner rooms, large *iwan* and a pillared porch, all still entirely Persian in feeling (fig 21). In the 16th and 17th centuries more pavilions were added, among them the Baghdad Kiosk (1639). This was designed as a domed hall in its upper part, with small corner rooms. It has a portico under a projecting roof, and kitchens and living rooms for the janissaries and court personnel, all in an arrangement owing more to chance than design and most delightfully set out with trees and garden beds.

Town caravanserai were no longer on the Seljuk pattern but rather of the Mamluk type with multi-storeyed arcaded courts, the lower rooms serving as warehouses and stables, the upper as dwelling rooms; many had several courtyards. After the Ipek Han in Brusa, built by Murad II in the fifteenth century, followed a number of stately 16th century hostels in Stambul; as a later

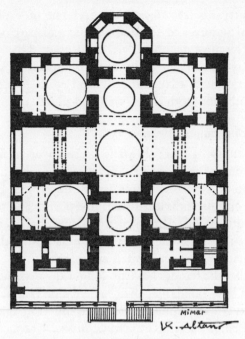

21. Ground plan of the Chinili Köshk in Istanbul, surveyed by K. Altan (cf. E. Kuhnel, *Die Sammlung türkischer und islamischer Kunst*, Berlin, 1938, fig 1). The correct reading of the date of building gives 1472, not, as in most authors, 1466.

example the magnificent domed complex of Asad Pasha Han in Damascus (1752) deserves to be singled out. On the other hand the bazaar markets (*besestan*), some of them very old, had no inner courts but had long aisles and crossings each of which was roofed with a small cupola, like the Ulu Jami' in Brusa (cf. plate 75a). Important baths are the large thermae of Eski and Yeni Kapliha near Brusa, the former still 14th century, the latter of the time of Sulayman the Magnificent, with imposing dome chambers arranged to a strict plan following that handed down from antiquity.

An important feature in Ottoman secular architecture is the fountains (*sebil*) which were a favourite form of public endowment in the capital. They have much in common with the fountains in mosque courtyards (*shadriwan, hanefiye*) but they often reached monumental stature and formed an essential part of the town's character. The most delightful are those erected by Ahmed III at Bab i Humayun, at Asab Qapu and at Top Hane, shaped like a pavilion, articulated architecturally and with protecting eaves, skilfully combining both draw-well and piped jets.

Ottoman Architectural Decoration

The continuity of Turkish art is more apparent in decorative details than in the mastery of constructive problems, and often the evolution of Ottoman forms can be traced step by step from their Seljuk origins. Individual parts like portals and prayer niches are not essentially different from the forms characteristic for the Konia period; the stalactite motif is dominant in both and is only used more widely here on capitals and brackets.

It is true that the façades have no longer the decorative function they had on state buildings; their articulation is much more dictated by structural requirements, and thus the marble facing, when it is used, is more architectonic in so far as the flat and discrete ornament is confined to details like window frames and spandrels, within a rather bald, broad articulation. Facings play an important part in mosques and tombs as well as in palaces and fountains; even the *minbar* is now usually made of marble instead of the traditional wood and sometimes in state rooms the wall niches for the display of show objects, which used to be of wood, are sunk into marble panels. Ornamental stucco also retained its importance from the 15th to 18th centuries.

But the main share of interior decoration is still given to ceramic, often now used in a new way. The faience mosaic, which reached such brilliance in Konia, seems to have fallen into oblivion in the Brusa period, and its place taken by rich tile decoration. Blue glazed hexagonal tiles with gold designs and polychrome square ones with waxed cord outlines make an impressive decoration on the Green Mosque (Yeshil Jami') and the 'Green Turbe' which take their names from the ceramic which once covered their domes and minarets. These tiles were also used on the sarcophagi of the Sultans there. In the Chinili Köshk the old faience mosaic had a last transitory revival, presumably inspired by Persian architects, in the decoration of the *iwan*, while in the interior monochrome Brusa tiles came into their own.

A new development in tile ceramic set in with the foundation of the Iznik (Nicaea) faience industry. The book artists summoned by Selim I from Tebriz were among those to whom was commited the task of providing patterns for the wall facings needed in the mosques and palaces of Constantinople; the new typically Ottoman style of decoration soon manifested itself alongside the motifs adopted from Persia (arabesques, cloud bands, lotus palmettes etc). This was based on naturalistic plant patterns: tulips, hyacinths, carnations, roses, vines, pomegranates in symmetrical and well-balanced compositions. Technically, the difference between these and Iranian ceramics is considerable: the tiles combined into larger fields with borders are, as a rule, glazed white and painted mainly in cobalt blue, turquoise and tomato red, the latter colour in a unique reddish-brown shade and always slightly raised in relief. This was the favourite material for facing prayer niches in mosques and fireplaces in houses (cf. plate 77); the motifs in the Ahmediye, the *turbe* of Selim II and several rooms of the Old Saray are exceptionally charming; some mosques, like that of Rustem Pasha, were completely tiled inside, giving a delightfully unified, colourful effect.

Wood, the essential material for secular work, often received artistic treatment by carving, turning and painting; painting was practised particularly in Syria in *qaʿa*, and in Constantinople. Lacquering was not always used purely for abstract ornament, but was sometimes decorated with figures in a style close to that of the miniatures. On doors and wall niches the standard Seljuk carving gradually gave way to inlay of other woods, mother-of-pearl, ivory etc. Coloured glass was used in the stucco windows, sometimes in decorative patterns; exceptionally glass mosaic was still done, a reminiscence of the Byzantine tradition.

Turkish Rococo

An approximation to ideas of the European baroque can already be seen in the curves of the roofing and in details of the plant

12

decoration on the public fountains of the time of Ahmed III. Then when the French rococo style became known in Constanti-nople in the middle of the 18th century it immediately found an enthusiastic reception both at court and with the artists, who saw no future in the Ottoman tradition. They did keep to the struc-tural forms they had preserved, but executed the decorative parts of buildings and details of decoration in a spirit which fully en-titles us to speak of a Turkish rococo. For even though it was Western craftsmen who broke the ground for the new taste, the native artisans soon followed them, and it is extraordinary to see with what understanding they penetrated a world of forms which until then had been alien to them.

The clearest example of the change is seen in the mosque of Nur-i-Osmaniye built between 1748 and 1755. The forecourt is startling with its semi-circular layout fronted by porticoes, and there are other original departures from the traditional building forms; but the most interesting is the attempt to replace the stalac-tite structure of the portal niches with parallel projecting friezes of acanthus leaves, fixed over baroque brackets. Similarly, but much more radically rococo, are the shapes of fireplaces and wall niches in some rooms of the Old Saray, and the walls and ceilings decorated with gilded stucco. In furnishings this change of style had even more far-reaching consequences; European arm-chairs, sofas, grandfather clocks were now introduced into the imperial apartments.

Since this time a rococo flavour has lingered in Turkish secular architecture, in more bombastic shapes and in stricter design, and it has spread from Istanbul into the country. For example it has influenced the tomb stones, and can be seen in various fields of craftwork; curtains and other embroideries used in interior decoration bring it once again into the architectural sphere.

The imperial palaces built on the Bosporos in the 19th century are connected at least in details with this phase, though they all bear the Western stamp without any viable new style to replace the native tradition they have virtually thrown overboard. They are to be valued up to a point as a classical reaction: Beilerbey, Dolma Baghtje, Chiragan Saray and lastly Yildiz Kiosk. They are the first stages in the gradual complete and deliberate Europeanization of Turkish domestic architecture.

Ottoman Books

The school of calligraphy and illumination of Constantinople was a daughter foundation of the school of Tebriz; Persian masters prepared the ground for the flowering of all branches of the craft of book-making, and their influence remained so strong that criteria are often lacking to decide between Persian and Turkish work. The most outstanding work is again in luxury copies of the Koran, of which there is a splendid collection in the Museum of Turkish and Islamic Art in Istanbul. Some are by famous calligraphers whose renown was widespread, especially for their work in Thuluth, in the Ottoman period. They also provided texts for decorating mosques, for epitaphs etc. Among their most distinguished tasks in their service to the court chancellery was the provision of completed edicts and commissions (*firman*) with a heading decorated with the ornamental cypher of the Sultan (*tughra*). The illuminators prided themselves in devising constant new variations for decorating the promulgations of their sovereign; arabesques and flowers were the chosen means of heightening the decorative effect. The text itself of the document, often a yard-long scroll, began under the *tughra* and was written in the customary chancellery hand with lightly upward swinging characters, frequently in gold or coloured inks.

The Sultans were zealous to establish calligraphy in every way possible as the most noble of all arts, and many of them took pride in being themselves recognized by the guild as masters of calligraphy.

Book illuminators used not only the same motifs but the same colours as the masters of the Safavid period, and their display pages often surpass the splendour of their models. A Turkish speciality which was widely adopted was a small pocket-size Koran. The bindings are closely allied to Persian work. Blind and gold tooling, cut-outs in leather and paper filigree, and lacquer were restricted to ornamental and epigraphic motifs.

Copies of the Persian epics were much in vogue, and,

notwithstanding Sunnite scruples, the miniature painting to illustrate them was taken over as well. It was long practised by the Constantinople masters in strict subservience to its models, although an independent tradition of Turkish painting existed since before the Timurid period. The history of the Ottoman school of painting is still obscure; but at all events it was already in existence when Sultan Muhammad the Conqueror summoned the famous Venetian painter Gentile Bellini to his court to guide the art into new paths. Special tasks were set by the illustration of historical works on the life and deeds of the sovereign, and here again Western influences made themselves felt. However, European models left no lasting stimulus.

Textiles and Embroidery

While Seljuk period textiles from Asia Minor are relatively rare, we have many examples from the Ottoman period, though only from the 15th century onwards. Brusa, the new capital, seems to have taken the lead in production, and silk brocades, velvets and brocade velvets were made which introduced a new stylistic orientation, related to Late Gothic Italian cloths both as to technique and designs, and competing from the 16th century onwards with the Venetian and Spanish wares on the European market. Ottoman naturalistic floral patterns prevailed here too, and Persian influences contributed to a stronger oriental note which ultimately supplanted all reminiscences of Western design. The ogival compartment is often retained, or in other cases the motifs are placed within parallel wavy bands or separately in continuous repeats. Carnations and tulips are made into palmettes, other flowers formed into rosettes; lanceolate leaves, pomegranates and various bud forms also appear, as well as the arabesques, cloud bands, crescents and other abstract devices (plate 78b).

The few vestment cloths surviving from the 15th century have patterns on a very large scale, while in the 16th century they are in closer repeat. The colour schemes of this epoch are extraordinarily rich, and textiles had many uses. They served for dress coats and other clothing, for table-cloths, saddle-cloths, curtains, and with less rich decoration for shrouds and banners. Elongated cushion covers with a fitted design of one large motif in the field and two narrow borders are known as Scutari covers and were much in demand, even in the West; it is not certain that they were actually produced on the Anatolian side of the city.

For the state tents, such as were perpetually in demand for the Turkish military leaders in the Balkan wars and were often set out with the most luxurious fittings, linen was used with bright coloured decoration sewn on, often very fine and tasteful appliqué; examples of these have reached German collections as 'Turkish booty'. Embroidery with gold and silver thread on velvet was much in vogue in the 17th century, and then soon came into the sphere of the new rococo style.

Anatolian Carpets

Between the Seljuk rugs already mentioned and the oldest surviving examples from the Ottoman period, which are of the second half of the 15th century, there is a gap which we can only partially fill by reference to the examples portrayed in early Dutch school and a few Italian paintings. There may well have been intermediary types of which by chance no record remains.

The nearest approach to a connection is afforded by a group which is reminiscent of Turkoman work in the geometric motifs of the pattern of the field, in its dark colouring, and in the Kufic script on the borders. They are called Holbein rugs because they appear in the pictures of the great German painter, though they appear earlier (by 1451) quite frequently in Italian pictures, and the originals themselves are not rare (plate 79a). A related pattern with rather larger motifs in livelier colours was especially favoured by the Flemish masters, though also known to Holbein and some Italians, and another variant, with geometric arabesques, always yellow on a red ground, is related to the Ushak type.

This in its most usual form has similarities with the Persian medallion designs, or sometimes there are large and small stars in the field (plate 79b); the border is of cloud bands, fragments of calligraphy or symmetrically placed floral motifs. The colour scheme—mainly light blue, dark blue and red with yellow outlines—is very strong and harmonious, and in this group, which is the one that appears most frequently after the mid-16th century in Dutch pictures, we meet the first examples of the prayer rug, with a single or double *mihrab* niche. These became characteristic of Anatolia. There are two variants of the Ushak style: rugs with a white ground and a single motif repeated over the whole field, and the so-called 'Seven burgher rugs' which are met with in such amazingly large numbers in Transylvanian churches that the assumption seems justified that they were specially manufactured for export to Hungary and Rumania. They too are frequently represented in 17th century paintings and so can be exactly dated.

Besides these classic types of Anatolian rug-making, there is a class which has been made since the mid-16th century in a particular factory, which is markedly different in technique and design from the groups already mentioned. Their place of manufacture was not discovered until recently. They constitute in colour scheme, material and knotting technique a direct continuation of the Mamluk rugs made in Cairo (see p. 124), and it is now certain that the majority of them came from Egypt and a smaller quantity from workshops transplanted from there to Anatolia. The designs are mainly based on naturalistic floral motifs, as was characteristic for all the arts in the flourishing period of the Ottoman style. In the buoyant line drawing with its reminiscences of Persian rugs of this period, we can recognize them as the work of a court industry, in contrast with the folk-art character of the other groups with their much stiffer and more deliberately drawn patterns. Many of them are among the finest examples of knotting known, the velvety texture rivalling the best Indian work. Prayer rugs with the *mihrab* niche motif were favoured in this type as well, the motif receiving especially stylish treatment (plate 80).

The Giordes, Ladik, Kula Melas, Bergama and other variants in demand in the trade are all products of an industry already decadent even in the early 19th century, which was making serviceable but artistically undisciplined pieces in which neither the ornament nor the contrast of field and border is understood. In the later Ushak style a type arose which was much sought after in Europe, particularly in the 18th century, in spite of the loose and far from durable knotting. These so-called Smyrna rugs were ordered in large batches. From them a further branch of modern Anatolian manufacture developed.

Ottoman Crafts and Ceramics

The Istanbul museums possess a large number of very varied Koran chests, and also Koran desks (*rahle*) and similar mosque equipment of the 16th to 18th centuries, decorated with inlay of ivory, mother-of-pearl etc. This technique was then used on secular objects such as chairs and stools, and in the 19th century led to the production in Istanbul and Damascus of large quantities of such furniture for the bazaars.

Three main groups are to be distinguished in the ceramic vessels produced in the best period of Ottoman art, all with a hard body and decorated under the glaze. The oldest group begins as early as the 15th century, it has cobalt blue decoration of finely drawn and close floral scrolls, with arabesques and inscriptions on a white ground. Besides dishes, bowls, ewers, we often find mosque lamps in this ware. They were required as substitutes for the older Syrian ceremonial pieces of enamelled glass. It has not yet been decided whether Kutahia was the source of these elegant Turkish wares; but it cannot be doubted as the home of the second category, which it was previously the custom to call 'Damascus faience'. The wares have a white ground decorated in blue, turquoise, green, aubergine, and other colours with the whole wealth of the Ottoman plant designs (tulips, carnations, roses, hyacinths, lilies, grapes, artichokes, cypresses) besides much stylized abstract ornament, on vases, jugs, plates and dishes. The same colour scheme and similar patterns are also found on later tiles, which most notably decorate the mosques of Damascus, and it is this circumstance which has led to the ascription of this purely Turkish ware to the Syrian capital.

Iznik, the undisputed home of the tiles used to face walls in Istanbul, is perhaps also in fact the home of the two abovementioned classes, as it certainly is of the third type of Turkish table ware which, following a wayward tradition, is still erroneously called Rhodes faience. Its forms and patterns are in general closely similar to those of the wares mentioned, the repertoire enlarged by very typical tumbler-like flower pots and by sailing boats, animal figures and other animate motifs (plate 78a). In the palette it has the clay-based brownish red, mentioned before as characteristic of facing tiles, instead of aubergine. In the 18th century production declined in Iznik, while Kutahia received a slight stimulus from the manufacture of small utility wares such as cups, inkpots, plates, in vivid colours. This continued into the 19th century, declining into a poor peasant ceramic made with the participation of Armenian potters.

As in the Safavid period in Persia, bronze utensils fell right into the background; silver inlay was no longer practised in the Ottoman period and nothing of interest was produced, apart from openwork mosque lamps, usually in the shape of houses or tents with domed roofs, copied from the type usual in Cairo in late Mamluk times.

But in weapons the Turkish craftsmen soon rivalled the Persian, who here again had shown them the way. Great numbers of interesting examples have reached European collections as booty from the Turkish wars. The sabre blades are outstanding for the quality of their steel, they were taken as models for Western cavalry weapons. In the 17th century hilts and sheaths of daggers were often decorated with arabesques or flowers in transparent enamel, and 'buzogany' were used as clubs, with a smooth pear-shaped body. The long-handled battle-axe was also known, and the double axe which was primarily the badge of office of the commander. Parts of armour of various kinds for men and horses were often richly decorated with inlay, stirrups and horse bits sometimes finished in artistic openwork, the horses' bridles plated with engraved silver or with gilt bronze and glass paste. The characteristic shape of helmet was the Ottoman pointed and ribbed ogival headpiece, which was introduced into Hungary and Poland during the Turkish wars and is known to us by the Hungarian word *schischak*. Another type imitated the earlier felt cap of the Janissaries which derived from dervish caps, and like these was equipped with the now customary plumes in plume holders. Shields were mostly round, of concentric reed work and with a massive boss.

1a. Northern side of the arcaded courtyard of the Great Mosque in Damascus, with minaret. Umayyad, 7th century. Photo: Prof. Creswell.

1b. The pillared hall of the 'Amr Mosque in Old Cairo (founded in 642, first extension in 673). Umayyad, 7th–8th century.

2a. The exterior of the garrison mosque of Sidi 'Oqba in Qairawan (founded 670, several times destroyed in the 8th century, rebuilt in 821, enlarged in 894).

2b. The court façade and sanctuary of the Mosque of Sidi 'Oqba in Qairawan. The domes over the transept 8th–9th century. From H. Saladin, *La mosquée de Sidi Okba à Kairouan.*

3. Interior of the third extension of the Umayyad mosque in Cordova, under the
chancellor al-Mansur, after 990.

4. Dome chamber in front of the *mihrab* of the mosque of the Umayyads in Cordova, associated with the second extension under the Caliph al-Hakam II, 965–970. Photo: Garzón, Granada.

5. The Dome of the Rock (Qubbat as-Sakhra, Mosque of 'Omar) in Jerusalem, late
7th century, built by the Caliph 'Abdelmalik.

6. Triangle J from the left-hand façade of Mshatta in Transjordania. Early 8th century, now in the Islamic Museum, Berlin. Museum photograph.

7. Decoration on the right-hand half of the façade of Mshatta. Early 8th century. Triangle S. Photo: Islamic Museum, Berlin.

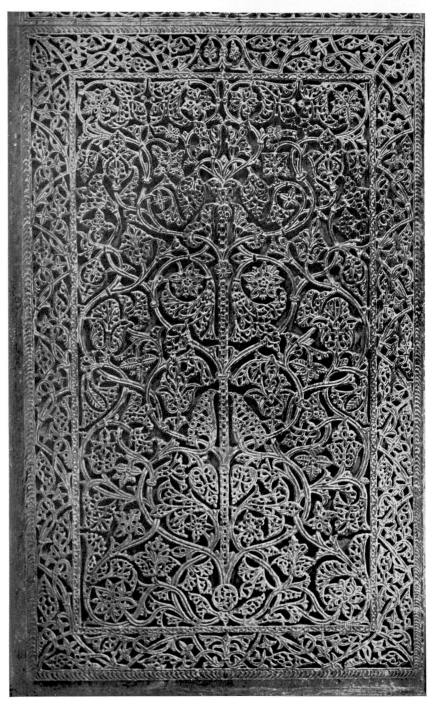

8. Marble facing, with ornamental carving, near the *mihrab* of the Umayyad mosque in Cordova. c. 970. Photo: Garzón, Granada.

9. Architectural fantasy motif in the mosaic decoration of the court of the Great Mosque in Damascus, early 8th century.

10. *Minbar* (pulpit) in the Mosque of Sidi 'Oqba in Qairawan, of plane-tree wood with rich carving in the Umayyad style, Baghdad work. Set up by Ibrahim ibn al-Aghlab in the 9th century when the mosque was enlarged.

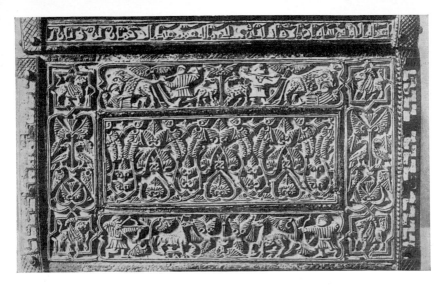

11a. Narrow side of the carved ivory chest from the Cathedral of Palencia in the Archaeological Museum in Madrid. Cuenca (Spain), dated 1049/50.

11b. Marble ablution basin, from Madinat az-Zahra, in the Archaeological Museum, Madrid. Cordova, dated 987.

12a. Ivory pyx with figured carving, made for the Umayyad prince al-Mughira. Cordova, dated 968. Louvre, Paris. From G. Migeon, *Musée du Louvre: L'Art musulman.*

12b. Page from a Kufic Koran on parchment, Iraq(?). 9th century, Museum Dahlem, Berlin. Photo: Islamic Department.

13a. Enclosure wall of the Great Mosque in Samarra with the 'Malwiye', 846–852 under the Caliph al-Mutawakkil. Photo: Islamic Museum, Berlin.

13b. The complex of the Ibn Tulun Mosque in Cairo, 877–879. Photo: Lehnert & Landrock, Cairo.

14. View into the sanctuary of the Ibn Tulun Mosque in Cairo, with pointed arches on brick piers and stucco ornament, 877–879.

15. Niches with stucco dado in a room of the castle of Balkuwara, near Samarra, 854–859. Photo: Islamic Museum, Berlin.

16a. Lustre bowl with representation of a camel, so-called Samarra ware, Iraq. 9th-10th century, in the Louvre, Paris. Photo: BAP, Paris.

16b. Two dancing girls, wall-painting from the Caliph's palace in Samarra, mid-9th century. From Herzfeld, *Die Malereien von Samarra*, Plate II.

17a Silk cloth (shroud) with pairs of ibex (detail), Persia, dated 998, in the Art Museum, Cleveland, USA. Photo: Mallon. Cf. Wiet, *Soieries persanes*, 1948, No. III.

17b. Silk cloth with pairs of lions, Persia, 10th century (detail), in the Museo Sacro, Vatican.

18a. The Bab en-Nasr gateway in the Fatimid town fortifications of Cairo, 1087–1093, exterior view.

18b. Bab el-Futuh in Cairo from the inside, joined on to it the Fatimid fortification wall (1087–93). Photo: Prof. Creswell.

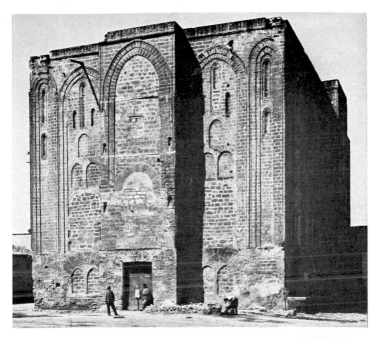

19a. Norman castle of Cuba in Palermo, built in 1180 by William II.
Photo: Anderson, Rome.

19b. Façade of the Hakim Mosque in Cairo, c. 1000. From Creswell,
Muslim Architecture in Egypt, I.

20a. Courtyard of the Mosque of Azhar in Cairo, late 10th century. Photo: Lehnert & Landrock, Cairo.

20b. Groups of students with their teachers in the Mosque of Azhar. Photo: Lehnert & Landrock, Cairo.

21. Ornamental panels with carved figure motifs from the Fatimid Western Palace, now in the Islamic Museum Cairo, 11th–12th century. From G. Wiet, *Album du Musée Arabe*, plate 22.

22a. Ivory horn (so-called oliphant) with carved animal motifs, in the Museum Dahlem, Berlin. Egypt or Southern Italy, 11th century. Photo: Islamic Department.

22b. Openwork plaque of ivory with figured carving in the Museo Nazionale, Florence (one of a series). Egypt, 11th–12th century. Photo : Bruckmann, Munich.

22c. Decoration on the door of the church of La Marto-rana in Palermo. Egypt or Sicily, mid–12th century. Photo: Brogi.

23a. Tiraz cloth with silk embroidery on linen (detail), in the Kunstgewerbemuseum, Berlin. Egypt, 12th century. Museum photograph.

23b. Ivory chest with painting in the Cathedral of Triento. Sicily, 13th century. Venturi, *L'Arte*, Vol. XIII.

24b. So-called Hedwig goblet of cut glass with decoration, in the Rijksmuseum, Amsterdam. Egypt or Syria, 12th century. Photo: H. Prell, Amsterdam.

24a. Handled jug of rock crystal in the Hermitage, Leningrad (formerly Stroganoff collection, Rome). Egypt, 11th century.

25. Bronze figure of a griffin (incense vessel?) with engraved ornament and inscriptions, in the Camposanto at Pisa. Egypt, 11th–12th century (allegedly booty from a crusade).
Photo: Brogi, Florence.

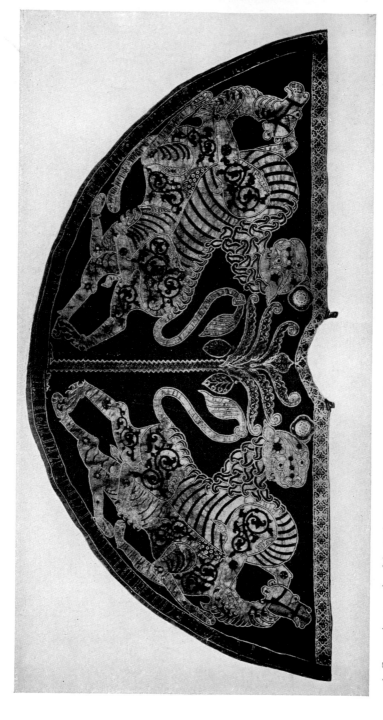

26. Coronation mantle of the Holy Roman Emperors, originally made for King Roger II of Sicily in the court workshop of Palermo in the year 1133 (according to the Arabic border inscription). Embroidery in gold with pearls on a red ground with mirror repeat motif (lions attacking camels) in the Fatimid style. In the Schatzkammer of the Hofburg, Vienna.

27b. Funerary tower in Radkan near Qutshan (Persia), round with conical roof, c. 22 metres high, with two gates. Dating incomplete. 13th century. From Diez, *Churasanische Baudenkmäler*, plate 6.

27a. Funerary tower Gunbed-i-Qabus in Gūrgan, built, according to an inscription, for the Ziyarid prince Sham al-Ma'ali Qabus (976–1012), by himself during his lifetime, dated by v. Berchem to 397 H (A.D. 1006/07). (The dating is not clear.) A ten-sided brick building, about 10 metres high. From Diez. *Churasanische Baudenkmäler*, plate 4.

28a. 'Mausoleum of Sitta Zubaida', wife of the Caliph Harun ar-Rashid, near Baghdad, with *muqarnas* dome and faceted surround. The traditional ascription is questionable, since the lady is supposed to have been buried in Qazimain near Baghdad. If the building was originally erected in the 9th century, it was completely renovated in the 13th.

28b. Domed tomb of the Theologian al-Ghazali (d. 1111) in Tus (Khorasan). 12th century. From Diez, *Churasanische Baudenkmäler*, plate 20.

29. Entrance to the citadel of Aleppo, which was built in 1170 by Nur ed-din, completed by Saladin and restored in the 13th century.

30a. Portal of the Seljuk Laranda Mosque (also called Sahib Ata) in Konia, dated 1258, originally flanked by two minarets, of which only one remains. From Sarre, *Denkmäler persischer Baukunst*.

30b. Minaret of the Mosque of Sultan Qutb ed-din Aybak (1206–1210), founder of the dynasty of the so-called Slave Kings in Hindustan, with their seat in Delhi. The deeply fluted tower tapers towards the top, with interrupting galleries and horizontal rings of decorative inscriptions in Kufic and Naskhi, 72·5 metres high.

31. Portal of the Seljuk Mosque in Diwrigi (Asia Minor), dated 1228, with rich
sculptural ornament. From Glück and Diez, *Die Kunst des Islam*, plate VIII.

32. Seljuk wooden door, single, from Karaman (Asia Minor). 13th century, in the Museum in Ankara. Cf. E. Kühnel, *Türkische und islamische Kunst im Tschinili Köschk* (Berlin 1938), plate 11. Photo: Istanbul Museum.

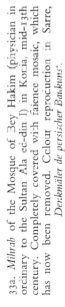

33b. Wooden *minbar* of the Ala ed-din Mosque in Konia, with rich carving and panelling, dated 1155.

33a. *Mihrab* of the Mosque of Bey Hakim (physician in ordinary to the Sultan Ala ed-din I) in Koria, mid-13th century. Completely covered with faience mosaic, which has now been removed. Colour reproduction in Sarre, *Denkmäler de persischer Baukuns'*.

34. *Mihrab* (blind niche) of lustre tiles from the Meidan Mosque in Kashan (Persia), dated 1226, by the potter al-Hassan ibn 'Arabshah. Islamic Museum, Berlin. Museum photograph.

35a. Erasistratos and his Amanuensis: miniature from an Arabic translation of Dioscorides' *Materia Medica*, dated 1224, written and illuminated by 'Abdallah ibn el-Fadhl; formerly in the library of S. Sophia, now scattered among a number of collections. The page reproduced here is in the Freer Gallery, Washington (formerly Sarre Collection, Berlin). Baghdad school. Photo: Islamic Museum Berlin.

35b. Passenger boat on the Tigris. Miniature from a manuscript of the 'Maqamen' of Hariri which depict the adventures and tricks of Abu Zayd of Seruj. In the Orient Institute, Leningrad. Baghdad school, c. 1230. Photo: Islamic Museum, Berlin.

36. Bronze vessel with copper and silver inlay in horizontal rings, with figure scenes and inscriptions (*inter alia* in 'animated' Naskhi), in the Hermitage, Leningrad. Dated 1163 in Herat (Khorasan). Photo: Bruckmann.

37b. Seljuk knotted carpet (detail) with geometric pattern and script border, from the Ala ed-din mosque in Konia, now in the Museum of Turkish and Islamic Art in Istanbul. Asia Minor, 13th century. Photo: Bruckmann.

37a. Bronze candlestick with silver inlay, with rows of standing figures, animal medallions and Christian scenes, executed by Daud ibn Salama in Mosul, dated 1238, in the Musée des Arts décoratifs, Paris. Photo: Bruckmann.

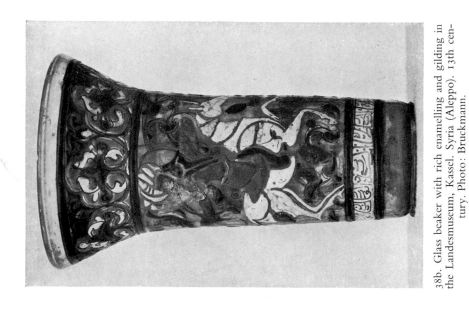

38b. Glass beaker with rich enamelling and gilding in the Landesmuseum, Kassel. Syria (Aleppo). 13th century. Photo: Bruckmann.

38a. Bottle in polychrome so-called Mínaí faience, formerly with Parish-Watson in New York. Persia (Rayy), c. 1200.

39. Gur Emir, the mausoleum of Timur in Samarqand, with tent-like banded dome on a high drum, faced with faience mosaic. Erected about 1500. From Sarre, *Denkmäler persischer Baukunst.*

40a. Dome and minaret of the Shir Dar Mosque in Samarqand, with faience mosaic, c. 1600.

40b. Mausoleum of the Mongol Sultan Uljaitu Khodabende in Sultania (Persia), built 1320. From Sarre, *Denkmäler persischer Baukunst*.

41. Faience decoration on the entrance to the mausoleum of Chojuk Bika, sister of Timur (d. 1371), in Samarqand. From H. R. d'Allemagne, *Du Khorasan au Pays des Bakhtiari*, Paris, 1911.

42b. Knotted carpet with dragon and phoenix in two compartments, Caucasus, c. 1400, in the

42a. Page from a luxury copy of the Koran in the Leipzig City Library, Baghdad (?), c. 1300. Photo: Bruckmann.

43a. Pair of stags. Miniature with Chinese influence from a bestiary (Manafi 'al-Hayawan) in the Pierpont Morgan Library in New York. Dated 1295 in Maragha (Persia). Photo: Pierpont Morgan Library.

43b. Departure of Hamza, the uncle, and 'Ali, the son-in-law of the Prophet Muhammad. Miniature in Mongol style from a manuscript of the *World Chronicle* of the Vizir Rashid ed-din in the Royal Asiatic Society, London. Persia (Tebriz school), dated 1314. From Martin, *Miniature Painting and Painters of Persia, India and Turkey*.

44a. Mongol–Turkish helmet with silver inlay in the Dahlem Museum, Berlin. West Turkestan or Turkey, 14th–15th century. Photo: Islamic Department.

44b. Nushirwan rewards the wise Buzurgmihr with sacks of gold. Miniature from a luxury copy of the Shah-nama, formerly in the possession of Demotte, New York. Persia (Tebriz school), c. 1330/40. Photo: Cooper, London.

45. Meeting of Humay and Humayun in the garden of the Imperial Palace in China. Single page from a lost manuscript in the Musée des Arts décoratifs, Paris. Persia, Timurid (Herat school), c. 1420/30. Photo: Bruckmann.

46. Façade, dome and minaret of the Mamluk Sultan Qalaun's group of buildings in Cairo, 1284/85.

47. Necropolis of the Mamluks before the gates of Cairo (so-called Tombs of the Caliphs), domed mausolea, mostly of the 15th century.

48. *Mihrab* wall and *minbar* (pulpit) in the al-Burdeini in Cairo. Its execution, 1616, falls in the Ottoman period, but both architecturally and in the style of decoration it is still completely Mamluk in character.

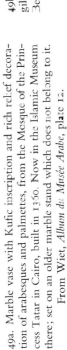

49a. Marble vase with Kufic inscription and rich relief decoration of arabesques and palmettes, from the Mosque of the Princess Tatar in Cairo, built in 1350. Now in the Islamic Museum there; set on an older marble stand which does not belong to it.
From Wiet, *Album du Musée Arabe*, plate 12.

49b. Mosque hanging-lamp of glass with enamelling and gilding. Inscriptions in large Naskhi. Dahlem Museum, Berlin. Syria (Aleppo), 14th century. Photo: Islamic Department.

50. Koran table (*kursi*) of bronze, with silver and gold inlay, partly
openwork, executed for Sultan Muhammad an-Nasir (1327),
probably from one of the mosques founded by him, now in the
Islamic Museum, Cairo.

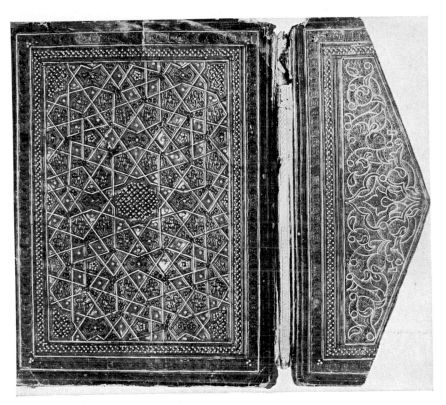

51a. Mamluk book binding with blind and gold tooling in the Islamic Museum, Berlin (formerly collection of Prof. B. Moritz). Egypt, 13th–14th century. Photo: Bruckmann.

51b. Bronze bowl with silver inlay: battle scene, animal frieze, inscription about a Mamluk Emir and official emblem, not yet satisfactorily interpreted. Museum Dahlem, Berlin (formerly Sarre collection). Photo: Islamic Museum.

52. Chinese gold brocade with pairs of birds (parrots?), dragons and medallions with an inscription about the Mamluk Sultan an-Nasir (d. 1340), for whom the cloth was made. It is questionable whether the cloth was manufactured in China itself or in the realm of the Golden Horde. In the Marienkirche, Danzig. First half 14th century.
Photo: Bruckmann.

53a. Interior of the Great Mosque in Algiers (on brick piers, with pointed horse-shoe and cusped arches). Almohad period, 12th century.

53b. Bab Agenau in Marrakesh, with stepped archivolts, arabesques and Kufic inscription. Almohad period, 12th century. From de Neizière, *Les monuments mauresques du Maroc.*

54. Earlier aspect of the minaret of the Great Mosque in Seville (now the cathedral), built in 1195 for the Almohad Abu Yaqub Yusuf. The upper section was destroyed by earthquake in 1355 and rebuilt quite differently in 1560/68 by Hernan Ruiz in Late Renaissance style, with a statue of Fides at the top which turned in the wind, giving the whole tower the popular appellation of 'Giralda'. The lower section with its geometric patterning remained as before. Relief of 1499 in the Villasena de Mena (Burgos).

55. Interior of the former synagogue (now the church of Sa. Maria la Blanca) in Toledo, with pine-cone capitals and wall decoration in Almohad style, 12th–13th century. Photo: Más, Barcelona.

56. View of the Lion Fountain through an arch giving an illusion of a succession of recessed arches, from one of the rooms of the *harim* of the Alhambra in Granada, with typical rich stucco decoration above a faience mosaic dado. 14th century.

57. Star-shaped rising stalactite dome with window lights above the so-called Sisters'
Hall in the *harim* complex of the Alhambra in Granada, 14th century. Photo: Garzón,
Granada.

58. Corner in the Court of Honour (so-called Maidens' Court) in the Alcazar in Seville, built by Peter the Cruel of Castile in place of the earlier Almohad residence, after 1350, with Moorish craftsmen (later much restored). Photo: Anderson, Rome.

59b. So-called 'Alhambra vase'; a large wing-handled vase of faïence, with rich lustre painting in script and abstract designs, from the Malaga factory. 14th century. Museo Nazionale in Palermo.

59a. Page from a fragment of the Koran written in Mahgrebi hand and illuminated in the Alhambra style in Granada or Fez in the 14th–15th century. Islamic Museum, Berlin. Museum photograph.

60. Corner of the great court of the Royal Mosque (Masjid-i-Shah) with rich faience mosaic decoration. Late 16th century. Photo: A. U. Pope.

61. One of the monumental bridges over the Zenderūd, designed as part of the town planning programme of Isfahan, widened into pavilions at each end and in the centre. Early 17th century. Photo: A. U. Pope.

62. Miniature by Behzad, from a manuscript of the History of Timur, signed top left, in the Gulbenkian Foundation in Lisbon. Persia (Herat), late 15th century.

63a. The Goatherd. Miniature by Riza 'Abbasi, Persia (Isfahan school), early 17th century. Leaf from a collection album, in the Leningrad Library. Note by the painter and signature cut off on left. Riza 'Abbasi has treated the same subject on another page, dated 1621 (formerly with Parish-Watson, New York).

63b. Calligraphic Persian motto in Ta'liq script with two figures in the corners and decorative stem scroll work. Formerly Cartier Collection, Paris. Persia, 16th century.

64a. Persian velvet brocade with repeat motif (beggar before a young man with a staff) in rich variety of colour. Persia (Kashan?) 17th century. Belongs to the so-called 'Turkish booty' in the Landesmuseum, Karlsruhe. Museum photograph.

64b. Persian so-called vase rug, about 1600 (detail), in the Österreichisches Museum für angewandte Kunst, Vienna.

65. Persian medallion carpet with garden landscape and animals, winged figures in the corners, strictly symmetrical in design (detail), probably from the court factory in Tebriz. Mid-16th century. In the County Museum in Los Angeles (formerly in the Mackay Collection, New York). A companion piece with identical design, but shortened at either end, was in the Islamic Department of the Berlin Museum, but was largely destroyed by war damage.

66. Persian, so-called Polish, rug, knotted in silk, with silver threads, from a court factory, probably Isfahan, about 1600. Evidently a gift from Shah Abbas I to a European court. Formerly in the Kestner Museum in Hanover, destroyed in the war. Photo: Kestner Museum.

67a. Interior of the Pearl Mosque (Moti Masjid) of the Moghul Emperor Shah Jehan, 1648–1655, built inside the Agra palace complex.

67b. The famous mausoleum of the Taj Mahal and its surrounding buildings, erected near Agra between 1630 and 1648 by the Emperor Shah Jehan, here reproduced in the very exact representation of an Indian miniature, from a collector's volume in the Museum Dahlem, Berlin (Indian Art Department). Photo: Islamic Museum, Berlin.

68a. The Diwan-i-Khas (private audience room) in Fatihpur Sikri, planned by the Emperor Akbar, a work of genius of Indian Islamic architecture, c. 1550, From Reuther, *Indische Paläste*.

68b. Frontage of the Great Mosque in Delhi, built c. 1644–1658 by the Emperor Shah Jehan, of red sandstone with marble inlay, inside extensive precincts with massive gatehouses. Considered to be the largest mosque in the Islamic world.

69. Jai Mandir, one of the state rooms in the palace at Amber, near Jaipur, in India, 17th century, with ornate decoration of mirror mosaic on walls and ceiling. Similar rich mirror mosaic decorated the Shish Mahal ('glass palace') in Lahore and other state rooms in the residences of the Mughal emperors of the 17th century. From Reuther, *Indische Paläste*, plate 82.

70. Architecturally planned park landscape with artificially meandering river, pavilions and small living blocks attached to one of the imperial residences. An example of the ideal landscapes of Mughal India. Miniature in an album in the Indian Art section of Museum Dahlem, Berlin. 17th–18th century. Photo: Islamic Museum, Berlin.

71. Emperor Jehangir riding on an elephant during a rhinoceros and gazelle
hunt, with his retinue. Various hunting episodes. India, Mughal school.
Early 17th century. Collection Otto Sohn-Rethel, Düsseldorf.

72a. Indian gazelle in the open. Indian miniature by the master painter Murad. Even more famous as an animal painter in the period of Jehangir (1605–1628) was Mansur, of whom a number of signed works survive. From an album in the Islamic Museum, Berlin. Museum photograph.

72b. Romantic landscape with a group of sheep stalked by a lynx. India, Mughal school of the 18th century. Islamic Museum, Berlin (from an album). Museum photograph.

73a. 'Vihagra Ragini', girl out walking, with a *vina*, an Indian musical instrument. The motif represents one of the 36 ragamala moods expressed in music. Formerly in the Museum für Völkerkunde, Berlin (now disappeared). Photo: Islamic Museum, Berlin.

73b. Krishna charming Gopis (shepherdesses) and cows with his flute. One of the favourite scenes from the Hindu Krishna legend. Miniature from one of the Rajput schools under influence of Mughal style. India, c. 1700. Museum of Fine Arts, Boston (A. Coomaraswamy Collection).

74. Knotted Indian picture rug, c. 1600. Composition in painting style
(living rooms, animals attacking, hunting expedition with ox-cart and
Indian leopard, fabulous animals etc, palmette border) in Boston Museum.
Museum photograph.

75a. View of the Ulu Jami' in Brusa with its separate domes, late 14th century.

75b. Mosque of the Sultan Bayazid in Istanbul, with forecourt and two minarets, built between 1501 and 1507 by the architect Kheir ed-din.

76. Interior of the Mosque of the Sultan Sulayman, with view of the *mihrab* and *minbar*.
Built 1550–1556 by Sinan. From Gurlitt, *Die Baukunst Konstantinopels*.

77. 17th century fireplace from a Turkish house, entirely covered with coloured tiles from Iznik. Victoria and Albert Museum, London. Museum photograph.

78a. Turkish faience bowl with blue decoration of flowers and inscriptions on a white ground. Iznik, 16th century. British Museum, London. Museum photograph.

78b. Turkish gold brocade with half-drop repeat of rows of groups of crescents, lanceolate leaves and other motifs on crimson ground. Brusa, 16th century. Musée des Arts décoratifs, Paris. Museum photograph.

79a. So-called Holbein rug with small pattern (detail), Asia Minor, c. 1500. Formerly in Islamic Museum, Berlin (now disappeared). Museum photograph.

79b. Ushak rug with star pattern (detail). Asia Minor (Ushak), 16th century. in the possession of Graf Dönhoff, Schlenderhan, near Cologne.

80. Prayer rug with triple niche, from the Ottoman court factory in Cairo, late 16th century. Egyptian work in Ottoman style. Metropolitan Museum, New York. Museum photograph.

Bibliography

General

KOECHLIN, R., L'art de l'Islam: La céramique (Musée des Arts décoratifs). Paris 1928
LANE, A., Early Islamic Pottery, and Later Islamic Pottery. London 1957
LAMM, C. J., Mittelalterliche Gläser und Steinschnittarbeiten aus dem Nahen Osten. Berlin 1930
FALKE, O. v., Kunstgeschichte der Seidenweberei. Berlin 1913
SCHMIDT, H., Alte Seidenstoffe. Brunswick 1958
KENDRICK, A. F., and TATTERSALL, C. E. C., Handwoven carpets, Oriental and European. London 1922
BODE, W. v., und KÜHNEL, E., Vorderasiatische Knüpfteppiche. 4th edn. Brunswick 1955
ERDMANN, K., Der orientalische Knüpfteppich, Tübingen 1955
SARRE, F., und TRENKWALD, H., Altorientalische Teppiche. Vienna–Leipzig 1926–28

The Applied Arts

CRESWELL, A., Early Muslim architecture. I. Umayyads. Oxford 1932
VOGUÉ, M. DE, Le temple de Jérusalem. Paris 1864
STRZYGOWSKI, J., Mschatta. Jahrb. d. preussischen Kunstsammlungen 1904
HERZFELD, E. E., Die Genesis der islamischen Kunst und das Mschattaproblem. Der Islam. 1910
—, Mschatta, Hîra und Bâdiya. Jahrb. d. preussischen Kunstsammlungen 1921
JAUSSEN et SAVIGNAC, Les châteaux arabes de Qeseir Amra, Haraneh et Tûba. Paris 1922
MUSIL, A., Kuseir Amra. Vienna 1907
SCHLUMBERGER, D., Les fouilles de Qasr el-Heir el-Gharbi. Syria 1939
HAMILTON, W., Khribat al-Mafjar. London 1959
PUTTRICH-REIGNARD, O., Die Palastanlage von Chirbet el-Minje. Palästina-Hefte des D. Vereins vom Hl. Lande. 1939
LÉZINE, A., Le ribat de Sousse. Tunis 1956
WULZINGER, K., und WATZINGER, C., Damaskus. Die islamische Stadt. Berlin 1924
SCHULZ, W. Ph., Die persisch-islamische Miniaturmalerei. Leipzig 1914
BLOCHET, E., Les peintures des manuscrits orientaux de la Bibliothèque Nationale. Paris 1914–20
BINYON/WILKINSON/GRAY, Persian Miniature Painting. London 1933
GRAY, B., Persische Malerei. Geneva 1961
SARRE, F., Islamische Bucheinbände. Berlin 1923
GRATZL, E., Islamische Bucheinbände. Leipzig 1924
RIVIÈRE, H., La céramique dans l'art musulman. Paris 1913

KOECHLIN, R., L'art de l'Islam: La céramique (Musée des Arts décoratifs), Paris 1928
LANE, A., Early Islamic Pottery, and Later Islamic Pottery. London 1957
LAMM, C. J., Mittelalterliche Gläser und Steinschnittarbeiten aus dem Nahen Osten. Berlin 1930
FALKE, O. v., Kunstgeschichte der Seidenweberei. Berlin 1913
SCHMIDT, H., Alte Seidenstoffe. Brunswick 1958
KENDRICK, A. F., and TATTERSALL, C. E. C., Handwoven carpets, Oriental and European. London 1922
BODE, W. v., und KÜHNEL, E., Vorderasiatische Knüpfteppiche. 4th edn. Brunswick 1955
ERDMANN, K., Der orientalische Knüpfteppich, Tübingen 1955
SARRE, F., und TRENKWALD, H., Altorientalische Teppiche. Vienna–Leipzig 1926–28

Umayyad Art

CRESWELL, A., Early Muslim architecture. I. Umayyads. Oxford 1932
VOGUÉ, M. DE, Le temple de Jérusalem. Paris 1864
STRZYGOWSKI, J., Mschatta. Jahrb. d. preussischen Kunstsammlungen 1904
HERZFELD, E., Die Genesis der islamischen Kunst und das Mschattaproblem. Der Islam. 1910
—, Mschatta, Hîra und Bâdiya. Jahrb. d. preussischen Kunstsammlungen 1921
JAUSSEN et SAVIGNAC, Les châteaux arabes de Qeseir Amra, Haraneh et Tûba. Paris 1922
MUSIL, A., Kuseir Amra. Vienna 1907
SCHLUMBERGER, D., Les fouilles de Qasr el-Heir el-Gharbi. Syria 1939
HAMILTON, W., Khirbat al-Mafjar. London 1959
PUTTRICH-REIGNARD, O., Die Palastanlage von Chirbet el-Minje. Palästina-Hefte des D. Vereins vom Hl. Lande. 1939
LÉZINE, A., Le ribat de Sousse. Tunis 1956
WULZINGER, K., und WATZINGER, C., Damaskus. Die islamische Stadt. Berlin 1924
CASANOVA, P. Essai de reconstruction topographique de la ville d'Al-Foustât, Le Caire 1916–19
ALY BAHGAT et GABRIEL, A., Fouilles d'Al-Foustât. Cairo 1921
VELÁZQUEZ BOSCO, R., Medina Azzahra y Alamiria. Madrid 1912
GÓMEZ MORENO, M., Arte árabe español hasta los Almohades. Ars Hispaniae III 1951
FERRANDIS, J., Marfiles árabes de Occidente. I. Madrid 1935
BECKWITH, J., Caskets from Cordoba. London 1960
SALADIN, H., La mosquée de Sidi Okba à Kairouan. Paris 1903

Abbasid Art

CRESWELL, A. C., Early Muslim Architecture. II. Abbasids. Oxford
GODARD A., Les anciennes mosquées de l'Iran. Athar-e Iran 1936
SARRE F., und HERZFELD, E., Archäologische Reise im Euphrat- und Tigris-Gebiet. Berlin 1911. 1920
REUTHER, O., Ocheidir. Leipzig 1912
BELL, G. L., Palace and mosque at Ukhaîdir. Oxford 1914
HERZFELD, E., Erster vorläufiger Bericht über die Ausgrabungen von Samarra. Berlin 1912
—, Der Wandschmuck der Bauten von Samarra. Berlin 1923
—, Die Malereien von Samarra. Berlin 1928

SARRE, F., Die Keramik von Samarra. Berlin 1925
LAMM, C. J., Das Glas von Samarra. Berlin 1928
HAUSER, W., and UPTON, J., The Iranian Expedition. Excavations at Nishapur. Bull. Metrop. Mus. 1937/38
PÉZARD, M., La céramique archaïque de l'Islam. Paris 1920
WIET, G., Soieries persanes. Cairo 1948

Fatimid Art

PRISSE D'AVENNES, L'art arabe d'après les monuments du Caire. Paris 1878
TARCHI, U., L'architettura e l'arte musulmana in Egitto. Turin 1922
BRIGGS, M. S., Muhammadan architecture in Egypt and Palestine. Oxford 1924
CRESWELL, A. C., Muslim Architecture of Egypt I: Ikhshids and Fatimids. Oxford 1952
BERCHEM, M. VAN, Notes d'archéologie arabe: Monuments et inscriptions fatimites. Journal Asiatique. Paris 1891
FLURY, S., Die Ornamente der Hakim- und Azharmoschee. Heidelberg 1912
MONNERET DE VILLARD, U., La necropoli musulmana di Aswân. Cairo 1930
—, Le pitture musulmane al soffitto della Cappella Palatina in Palermo. Rome 1950
BEYLIÉ, L. DE, La Kalaa des Beni Hammad. Paris 1909
ARATTA, G., L'architettura arabo-normanna in Sicilia. Milan 1913
WIET, G., Album du Musée Arabe. Cairo 1930
KÜHNEL, E., Islamische Stoff aus ägyptischen Gräbern. Berlin 1927
—, Die sarazenischen Olifanthörner. Jahrb. d. Berliner Museen I, 1959
FERRANDIS, J., Marfiles árabes de Occidente. II. Madrid 1940
COTT, P., Siculo-arabic ivories. Princeton 1939
MUSÉE DE L'ART ARABE, La céramique égyptienne de l'époque musulmane. Bâle 1922 (no text)

Seljuk Art

SARRE, F., Denkmäler persischer Baukunst. Berlin 1910
—, Seldschukische Kleinkunst. Leipzig 1909
DIEZ, E., Churasanische Baudenkmäler. Berlin 1918
—, Persien, Islamische Baukunst in Churasán. Hagen in Westphalia 1923
ERDMANN, K., Das anatolische Karavansaray I. Berlin 1961
GABRIEL, A., Monuments turcs d'Anatolie I, II. Paris 1931–34
MEYER-RIEFSTAHL, R., Turkish architecture in South-Western Anatolia. Cambridge, Mass. 1931
—, The Parish-Watson Collection of Mohammedan Potteries. New York 1922
STRZYGOWSKI, J., und BERCHEM, M. VAN, Amida. Heidelberg 1910
BACHMANN, W., Kirchen und Moscheen in Armenien und Kurdistan. Leipzig 1913
SARRE, F., und HERZFELD, E., Archäologische Reise im Euphrat- und Tigris-Gebiet. Berlin 1911. 1920
PREUSSER, K., Nordmesopotamische Baudenkmäler. Leipzig 1911
FLURY, S., Le décor épigraphique des monuments de Ghazna. Syria 1925
PAGE, J. A., An historical memoir on the Qutb: Delhi. Calcutta 1926

Persian Mongol Art

SARRE, F., Denkmäler persischer Baukunst. Berlin 1910
WILBER, D., The architecture of Islamic Iran: the Il Khanid period. Princeton 1955
COHN-WIENER, E., Turan: Islam. Baukunst in Mittelasien. Berlin 1930

STCHOUKINE, I., Les peintures des manuscrits timurides. Paris 1954
SCHUBERT v. SOLDERN, Z., Die Baudenkmale von Samarkand. Vienna 1898
KAIS. RUSS. ARCHÄOL. KOMMISSION, Les mosquées de Samarcande. I. Le Gour-Émir. St Petersburg 1905

Mamluk Art

Vgl. Fatimidische Kunst. Ferner:
CRESWELL, A. C., Muslim Architecture of Egypt II: Ayyubids and early Mamluks. Oxford 1960
HERZ-PASCHA, M., Die Baugruppe des Sultans Qalâûn in Kairo. Hamburg 1919
FOUQUET, D., Contribution à l'étude de la céramique orientale. Cairo 1900
SCHMORANZ, G., Altorientalische Glasgefäße. Vienna 1898
WIET, G., Lampes et bouteilles en verre émaillé (Musée Arabe). Cairo 1929
—, Objets en cuivre (Musée Arabe). Cairo 1932
ERDMANN, K., Kairener Teppiche. Ars Islamica 1938–40
KÜHNEL, E., Cairene Rugs (Textile Museum). Washington 1957

Moorish Art

KÜHNEL, E., Maurische Kunst. Berlin 1924
RICARD, P., Pour comprendre l'art musulman dans l'Afrique du Nord et en Espagne. Paris 1924
MARÇAIS, G., Manuel d'art musulman. L'Architecture: Tunisie, Algérie, Maroc, Espagne, Sicile. Paris 1926–27
DE LA NEIZIÈRE, Les monuments mauresques du Maroc. Paris 1922–23
TORRES BALBÁS, L., Arte Almohade, Nazari, Mudéjar. Ars Hispaniae IV, 1949
BASSET, H., et TERRASSE, H., Sanctuaires et forteresses almohades. Hesperis. 1924–26
JONES, O., and GOURY, J., Plans, elevations, sections and details of the Alhambra. London 1842
MARÇAIS, W. et G., Les monuments arabes de Tlemcen. Paris 1903
BASSET, H., et LÉVI-PROVENÇal, E., Chella, une nécropole mérinide. Hespéris. 1922
FROTHINGHAM, A., Lustreware of Spain. New York 1951
VAN DE PUT, W., Hispano-moresque ware of the XVth century. London 1904
—, Supplementary studies. London 1911

Safavid Art

SARRE, F., Denkmäler persischer Baukunst. Berlin 1910
SARRE, F., und MITTWOCH, E., Zeichnungen von Riza Abbasi. Munich 1914
MARTIN, F. R., Figurale persische Stoffe. 1899
STCHOUKINE, I., Les peintures des manuscrits safavis de 1502 à 1587, Paris 1959
Teppiche und Buchkunst: see General

Mogul Art

HAVELL, E. B., Indian architecture. London 1914
REUTHER, O., Indische Paläste und Wohnhäuser. Berlin 1924
BROWN, P., Indian painting under the Mughals. London 1923
GLÜCK, H., Die indischen Miniaturen des Haemzae-Romanes. Vienna 1915
KÜHNEL, E., und GOETZ, H. Indische Buchmalereien aus dem Jahângîr-Album d. Staatsbibl. zu Berlin. Berlin 1924
STRZYGOWSKI, J., Die indischen Miniaturen im Schlosse Schönbrunn. Vienna 1923
ARNOLD, T. W., and WILKINSON, J., The library of Chester Beatty: Indian miniatures. London 1936

COOMARASWAMY, A., Mughal Painting. Cambridge, Mass. 1930
GOETZ, H., Geschichte der indischen Miniaturmalerei. Berlin 1934
STCHOUKINE, I., La peinture indienne à l'époque des Grands Moghols. Paris 1929
HAJEK, T., Indian Miniatures of the Moghul School. London, Prague 1960

Ottoman Art

WILDE, H., Brussa. Berlin 1909
GURLITT, C., Die Baukunst Konstantinopels. Berlin 1912
GABRIEL, A., Les mosquées de Constantinople. Syria 1926
REUTHER, O., Die Qa'a. Jahrb. d. asiat. Kunst. 1925
MINETTI, H., Osmanische provinziale Baukunst auf dem Balkan. Hanover 1923
WULZINGER, K., WITTEK, P., SARRE, F., Das islamische Milet. Berlin 1935
OTTO-DORN, K., Das islamische Iznik. Berlin 1941
—, Türkische Keramik. Ankara 1960
BABINGER, F., Die großherrliche Tughra. Jahrb. d. asiat. Kunst. 1925
BURLINGTON FINE ARTS CLUB, Exhibition of the Fayence of Persia and the Nearer
    East. London 1908
RAYMOND, A., Alttürkische Keramik in Kleinasien und Konstantinopel. Munich
    1922

Index

DATE DUE

MAY 1 '67	DEC 3 '74		
MAY 22 '67	JAN 17 1977		
MAY 26 '67	OCT. 29. 1982		
OCT 11 '67	JUN. -2 1983		
MAY 28 '68	DEC. 10. 1984		
OCT 9 '68	DEC 19 1995		
MAY 17 '70			
APR 8 '77			